A CRITICAL EVALUATION

SMALL AND MEDIUM ENTERPRISES' TREND AND ITS IMPACT TOWARDS HRD

ALMAS SABIR

COLLEGE OF BUSINESS ADMINISTRATION
FACULTY OF BUSINESS & MANAGEMENT
UNIVERSITY OF HAIL, KINGDOM OF SAUDI ARABIA

SMALL AND MEDIUM ENTERPRISES' TREND AND ITS IMPACT TOWARDS HRD A CRITICAL EVALUATION

iUniverse books may be ordered through booksellers or by contacting:

iUniverse
1663 Liberty Drive
Bloomington, IN 47403
www.iuniverse.com
1-800-Authors (1-800-288-4677)

ISBN: 978-1-5320-6971-0 (sc)
ISBN: 978-1-5320-7014-3 (hc)
ISBN: 978-1-5320-6972-7 (e)

Print information available on the last page.

iUniverse rev. date: 03/22/2019

CONTENTS

CONCEPT

The 21st century is a time set apart by the speeding up and improvement in globalization and innovative trade. The monetary worldwide town free of any national limit has risen. For little and medium undertakings in India, the inquiries are how to take a few to get back some composure on world patterns and open doors for improvement, just as how to enormously advance and scan for leaps forward? These inquiries involve crucial concern. Under globalization, individuals will in general look for specialties in assets, and the outcome crosses national limits toward the most aggressive districts or nations. The quintessence of rivalry has changed from customary methods of efficiency to item quality, information, power, and advancement. Ventures in various nations demonstrate their solid motivating forces to create, select, and hold gifts. In the realm of free challenge, information and development must be enlarged to keep up focal points in monetary initiative.

The standard focus of this postulation to choose the Emerging Trend of Human Resource Development send in to limits their action or undertaking as consign to him/her in their individual recorded, post and portfolio and moreover to consider in nuances for research reason that what are the crucial needs require to change and to furthermore require base changing to enhance the effectiveness and efficiency for national interest and advancement of the economy, particularly in overall advancing circumstance.

As the world economy continues moving towards extended fuse, irrefutably the most unmistakable open entryways for Small-to-Medium Sized Enterprises (SMEs) will get from their ability to appreciate the overall business focus. It is generally recognized that SMEs are twisting up dynamically basic to the extent business, wealth creation, and the enhancement of improvement. In any case, there are broad inquiries regarding the idea of the board in this division with procedure makers suggesting that there are explicit inadequacies being developed, a nonappearance of cash related knowledge, advancing, imaginative vitality, sober minded learning, and human resource the officials. As needs be, various associations don't accomplish their most extreme limit and disregard to create.

HR has transformed into a settling part in SMEs and overseeing in various portions where HR has used and doing their work in independent techniques and propensities. Little of the monstrous composed works nevertheless, have focused on its effects upon used workforce either in the individual or in social event that may be past clear delineations and subsequently it requires the SMEs the board execution.

We dissect the creating thought of HR in SMEs divisions, examination the contemporary utilization of HR and its things and thusly our examination in like manner revolve around employment, and obligations of the SMEs with respect to the said title as picked at this paper. The investigation similarly takes a gander at the effect of HRD in the delegate's and how it fabricates the productivity and advantage and duty of the assignment of the endeavor. This examination also assesses the board's undertakings to 'incorporate' individuals in the itemizing of their own work system as disseminated to him/her in their specific region or archived. Starting now and into the foreseeable future, it is fantastic dynamic control of learning a long ways past of these Industries as whole and HR explicitly.

Shown analyze exhibits that how HR used in SMEs and how they associated with grow the SMEs prospects and where and how the issues can be changed? What are its present example and its activity in the India? It was one of the uncommon testing with helpful experiences as a researcher for us to explore, assemble the relevant information in all out structure that this title end up being especially captivating and with the true objective of the examination which this examination is being done at our end and going to consider hereunder and showed at this result in the last area. It is very huge subject for the examination that has been taken underwriting by the RDC by the stress master of the University and prepare at our end.

ACKNOWLEDGEMENT

It is a well-established fact that behind every achievement lays an unfathomable sea of gratitude to those who have extended their support and without whom this project would have ever come into existence. It gives me a great pleasure in acknowledging the invaluable assistance extended to me by various personalities in the successful completion of this dissertation.

I am indebted to Dr.Ali, Professor in School of Planning and Architecture, Delhi for his useful insights and valuable suggestions that he gave me during the preparation of this book. His unremitting inspiration and encouragement helped this book, to take the final shape.

Last, but not the least I am very thankful to my family members and my colleagues who have helped me to complete the book.

Dr Ali

FOREWORD

This book intends to improve the comprehension of patterns and difficulties in advanced business development at the worldwide dimension. It makes an association between business pursuers and author's research. The book abridges what is hot—every year—in advanced business, however with an attention on appearing something new to experts from a scholarly point of view.

In this book, DR. ALMAS has assembled a few points, bunching them in three Parts that could be viewed as the means of a book. The book concentrates mainly on the primary advanced frameworks' patterns attempting to look at small and medium enterprise issues, from an administrative viewpoint, expecting to achieve a wide range of officials, including those without a management foundation.

It is a test for any author to distinguish the most well-known advanced business points in some random year. Given this, condensing the huge writing in data frameworks, advanced showcasing, and small and medium enterprises issues and recognizing the most cutting edge wonders is a laborious errand. I compliment Dr. Almas for this book and look.

Dr. Ali

DECLARATION BY THE AUTHOR

I hereby declare that work reported in the book entitled "Small and Medium Enterprises' Trend And its Impact towards HRD" is an authentic record of my work carried out under the supervision of Dr. Ali. I have not submitted this work elsewhere. I am fully responsible for the contents of my book.

Dr. Almas Sabir
College of Business Administration,
University of Hail,
Kingdom of Saudi Arabia

CHAPTER - 1

INTRODUCTION

1.1 SMEs and the growth of economy

The Small and Medium Enterprises (SMEs) segment assumes a critical job towards financial improvement paying little respect to an economy's size. It makes business, expands generation base and offers help to substantial scale undertakings. Monetary restoration after the East Asian emergencies of 1990's and worldwide budgetary emergency of 2009 has constrained the arrangement creators to look towards more grounded household markets being driven by SMEs. The littler firms have reacted well to the deregulation and progression of exchange and venture routines.

The worldwide economy in the previous two decades has encountered changes that begin from new meanings of advancement and business. This is seen as item and administration quality, innovation expansion, deregulated financial structures and the developing challenge among nations. This has driven the gainful firms and economies to redo methodologies in accordance with the ideas of endogenous development models. This thusly inferred another worldview for SMEs in which they need to compel themselves to be progressively beneficial and productive.

The SME part assumes the job of engrossing more work serious generation forms. Subsequently, they can be believed to contribute more towards the financial advancement through decrease in joblessness. For example, Philippines has indicated huge steps throughout the previous two decades and SMEs speak to 99.6 percent of all organizations with absolute work constrain business commitment at 69.9 percent. Also, it represented 32 percent of the nation's Gross Domestic Product (GDP) 1. SMEs have prompted a change of horticulture drove economies towards industry and administrations for a domain where little and huge firms are coordinated and pull in more noteworthy remote speculation and guarantee stable terms of exchange.

This pattern can be seen in China, Korea, Singapore, and other industrialized economies. In the European Union (EU), SME segment utilizes 66% of absolute work compel. For EU's situation the key factor towards work in SMEs has been dedication and inspiration of worker's accessible preparing openings and expertise advancement. The SMEs have all the more as of late embraced refined Human Resource Development (HRD) methodologies for better execution in the medium to long haul. The human capital and learning as immaterial resources for SMEs are winding up progressively imperative in taking future speculation choices. As indicated by the demonstrative methodology received by the HRD procedure is isolated into four stages:

1. Clarity of firm targets
2. Evaluating the outer conditions
3. Choosing preparing routines having long haul results
4. Evaluating the results normally

As the world economy keeps on pushing toward expanded joining due to progresses in correspondences innovation, development in creating nations, and decreases in exchange boundaries, the absolute most noteworthy open doors for independent ventures will get from their capacity to take an interest in the worldwide commercial center. Inside the created and creating nations of the world, it is presently commonly acknowledged by approach producers at nearby, territorial and national dimension that little medium measured undertakings (SMEs) are winding up progressively essential as far as work, riches creation and the advancement of development.

There are significant questions about the nature of the board in this division, with approach producers recommending that there are specific shortcomings in advancement, absence of monetary sharpness, showcasing, pioneering style, commonsense learning, and human asset the board. Accordingly, numerous organizations don't achieve their maximum capacity and neglect to develop, bringing about lost employments and riches for their locale in which they are based.

A more critical take a gander at the authoritative life cycle hypothesis models uncovers that there are between three to five phases that most associations will experience. Four basic stages exist in the life of a SME where the stages are controlled by the timeframe the firm has been agent. The length of each phase to be as per the following: Stage 1 is the start-up stage and is 0-3 years in term; Stage 2 is the development stage and is 4-6 years in span; Stage 3 is the development stage and is 6-9 years in term; and Stage 4 being the steadiness stage is roughly 10+ years in term. Coupled to every one of these stages is an alternate arrangement of business qualities, challenges, administrative capacities, and innovative needs that private ventures should confront.

Approach producers need to genuinely take a gander at the development capability of SMEs. Considering this, there is a need to:

1. Attempt a nitty gritty examination of the administration of little firms as for the linkages between the proprietor administrator; their abilities (experience and aptitude); the assets accessible to the firm and the administration of these inward and outside assets; and the impact of the outer condition and how the business visionaries oversee change;
2. understand the territorial setting of the improvement of little firms in a fringe locale and the issues explicit to such firms;
3. Examine how strategies could be enhanced to make private companies increasingly proficient and viable in their administration procedures, to address their shortcomings and expand on their qualities.

Attributes of a little firm, which recognizes it from bigger firms:

1. Little firms are in every case shy of money which constrains their key alternatives;

2. Their way to deal with hazard and vulnerability isn't reasonable;
3. The proprietor administrator's qualities in a general sense impact the firm;
4. The little firm is viewed as a social element and regularly spins around close to home connections;
5. They require their business choices to give a brisk result to balance the money limitations;
6. On account of point 5 most of their choices are transient choices;
7. Little firms for the most part work in a solitary market offering a restricted scope of items and administrations;
8. Due to point 7, they end up over-dependent on a couple of clients who make them powerless against disappointment should a key client suspend working with the little firm.
9. Choices are increasingly judgmental, including less individuals and in this way made a lot snappier;
10. They are increasingly receptive to changes in the commercial center; and
11. They are less inclined to impact improvements in the commercial center yet can react or conform to changes in the commercial center a lot snappier than bigger firms.

With the coming of arranged economy from 1951 and the resulting mechanical strategy pursued by Government of India, the two organizers and Government reserved a unique job for little scale ventures and medium scale enterprises in the Indian economy. Due security was concurred to the two areas, and especially for little scale enterprises from 1951 to 1991, till the country received an arrangement of advancement and globalization. Certain items were held for little scale units for quite a while, however this rundown of items are diminishing because of progress in modern approaches and atmosphere.

Government of India which underscored wise utilization of remote trade for import of capital merchandise and data sources; work escalated method of creation; business age; non convergence of dispersion of monetary power in the hands of few (as on account of enormous houses); demoralizing monopolistic practices of generation and advertising; lastly compelling commitment to outside trade gaining of the country with low import-serious tasks. It was likewise combined with the arrangement of de-centralization of modern exercises in couple of topographical focuses.

It tends to be seen that all around; SMEs in India met the desires for the Government in this admiration. SMEs created in a way, which made it feasible for them to accomplish the accompanying goals:-

1. High commitment to local creation
2. Significant fare income.
3. Low speculation prerequisites.
4. Operational adaptability.
5. Location insightful versatility.
6. Low escalated imports.
7. Capacities to create fitting indigenous innovation.
8. Import substitution.
9. Contribution towards guard creation.
10. Technology – arranged enterprises.
11. Competitiveness in household and fare markets.

Because of globalization and progression, combined with WTO routine, Indian SMEs have been going through a transitional period. With backing off of economy in India and abroad, especially USA and European Union and improved challenge from China and a couple of ease focuses of creation from abroad numerous units have been confronting an extreme time.

Those SMEs who have solid mechanical base, global business viewpoint, focused soul and eagerness to rebuild themselves will withstand the present difficulties and turn out with sparkling hues to make their own commitment to the Indian economy.

Expanding rivalry and globalization, alongside the need to create quality items, best case scenario costs, have provoked the business to present new item advancement techniques with current innovation. The need to advance mechanically prevalent techniques for item improvement remains constant, particularly for players in the SME portion. The small and medium undertaking part is broadly viewed as the motor of the Indian economy. Little and medium ventures (SMEs) contribute essentially to modern, financial, mechanical and local advancement in all created and creating economies.

The Indian SME advertises is esteemed at $5 billion. The 11 million SME units, which make up the Indian SME part, produce more than 8000 items. These comprise 95% of every single mechanical unit and contribute 40% to modern yield. The SME part additionally assumes a noteworthy job in the advancement of enterprising aptitudes and structures a significant segment of the nation's fare income. The commitment of SMEs in the mechanical advancement of the nation has been striking. At the state level, the legislature has assumed a noteworthy job in guaranteeing development by setting up different establishments to help these areas, which incorporate small scale Industry Advancement Partnerships (SIDC) and a few Habitats for Enterprise Improvement (CEDs).

There are numerous establishments that at present help SMEs at the national dimension. These incorporate the National Exploration Advancement Partnership (NRDC) and the Agency of Indian Guidelines (BIS).

Notwithstanding, since the mid-1990s, Indian SMEs have been presented to exceptional challenge because of expanding globalization. This has made survival and development of this segment troublesome.

It may appear to be hard to acquire an exact meaning of little and Medium Enterprise. A few authors have propounded different definitions and clarifications with respect to what Small and Medium Enterprises are. Some have characterized SMEs dependent on the qualities of the business, for example, estimate, dimension of activities, kind of industry, resources utilized, and number of representatives, turnover, market, the executives or control of the business or a few others.

As has been seen from the up to referenced, there is no accord on the genuine meaning of Small and Medium scale undertakings (SMEs) as can be seen that, the two terms, Small and Medium are relative and they vary from industry to industry and nation to nation. The distinction among enterprises could be believed to be the distinction in capital prerequisites of every business, which those among nations could emerge because of contrast in mechanical association by nations at various phases of financial advancement. What may in this way be characterized as SME in a created nation can be viewed as an extensive scale venture in a creating nation utilizing accomplices as settled speculation and work of the work compel? It is vital likewise to perceive that definitions change after some time and thus, even in a creating nation, what was recently delegated SME could be viewed as an extensive scale industry when the amounts of important parachutes change amid the generation procedure.

In spite of the dissimilarity in the near meanings of SMEs, the venture have some normal qualities, first, among these is that, proprietorship and the board are then held by one individual/family and henceforth, choices are regularly emotional.

Furthermore, SMEs require Small Capital base by and large, paying little mind to the business and the nation where they are based. Anyway they are frequently experiencing issues in pulling in assets for extension because of which they need to depend intensely on close to home sources.

Thirdly, practically speaking, the administration owner barely separates his private reserve from the organization's assets and this to a great extent adds to the wastefulness and non-execution of numerous SMEs. For them, most SMEs work with work escalated innovation. They think that its less simple to solid from one product offering to something fundamentally unique; indeed, most SMEs tie their targets more near the product offering than to different issues, for example, the utilization of capital. In many SMEs, there is less authoritative separation, higher workers turn ever and higher work venture proportion.

At long last, the rate of business mortality is high, most likely because of reasons of low capital, insufficient, Market data, absence of connection between business life and that of advertiser and low dimension of activity, among different components.

By its less capital escalated and high work assimilation nature, SSI segment has made noteworthy commitments to business age and furthermore to provincial industrialization. This division is in a perfect world fit to expand on the qualities of our customary abilities and information, by mixture of advancements, capital and inventive advertising rehearses. This is the helpful time to set up activities in the little scale area. It might be said that the standpoint is sure, without a doubt promising, given a few shields. This desire depends on a basic element of the Indian business and the interest structures. The decent variety underway frameworks and request structures will guarantee long haul concurrence of numerous layers of interest for shopper items/advances/forms. There will thrive and very much grounded markets for a similar item/process, separated by quality, esteem included and refinement. This normal for the Indian economy will permit reciprocal presence for different assorted kinds of units. The special and defensive approaches of the Govt. have guaranteed the nearness of this area in a bewildering scope of items, especially in customer products. Be that as it may, the terror of the segment has been the deficiencies in capital, innovation and advertising. The procedure of advancement combined with Government bolster will thusly, pull in the imbuement of simply these things in the area.

Small industry segment has performed exceedingly well and empowered our nation to accomplish a wide proportion of modern development and broadening.

1.2   Justification behind Fare Advancement

The ability of Indian MSME items to contend in universal markets is reflected in a lot of about 34% in national fares. If there should arise an occurrence of things like readymade articles of clothing, cowhide merchandise, handled sustenance's, designing things, the execution has been exemplary both regarding esteem and their offer inside the MSME area while at times like games products they represent 100% offer to the all-out fares of the division. In perspective on this, send out advancement from the little scale division has been concurred high need in India's fare advancement methodology which incorporates improvement of systems, motivators for higher generation of fares, particular medicines to MSMEs in the market improvement subsidize, disentanglement of obligation disadvantage rules, and so forth. Results of MSME exporters are shown in worldwide displays free of expense under MSME-DO Umbrella abroad.

National Honors for Quality Items

So as to empower the little scale units for delivering Quality merchandise, National Honors for Quality Items are given to the exceptional little scale units, who have made critical commitment for enhancing nature of their items. The plan is being worked since 1986. Victors of National Honors get a Trophy, a Testament and a Money Prize of Rs.25, 000/ - ($559.6) National Honors empower Little Scale Enterprises units to create quality merchandise which further empowers them to go into fare showcase.

The execution of the SMEs Sector has been promising till date. On the off chance that satisfactory help is given by the Government towards promoting of SSI items, this division will expand business open doors just as win profitable outside trade.

Little and Medium Business Development Chamber of India

(SME Chamber of India) puts endeavors for the advancement and development of SMEs by arranging different exercises to achieve its goals. The Chamber gives data and direction to new and existing business visionaries in successfully overseeing and developing their business.

The Chamber has created key procedures to advance and bolster the SME division. The Chamber likewise offers significance to and urges SMEs to embrace imaginative thoughts and ideas for the advancement of their business. The Chamber composes numerous Seminars, Conferences, Workshops and Training Programs and other exchange limited time exercises to instruct and make mindfulness among the SMEs.

TABLE: Definition of MSMEs in India:-

Description	Micro Enterprises	Small Enterprises	Medium Enterprises
INR (Rs.)	Upto 2,500,000	above 2,500,000 & upto 50,000,000	above 50,000,000 & upto 100,000,000
USD($)	Upto 62,500	above 62,500 & upto 1,250,000	above 1,250,000 & upto 2,500,000
Manufacturing Enterprises – Investment in Plant & Machinery			

Description	Micro Enterprises	Small Enterprises	Medium Enterprises
INR (Rs.)	upto 1,000,000	above 1,000,000 & upto 20,000,000	above 20,000,000& upto 50,000,000
USD($)	Upto 25,000	above 25,000 & upto 500,000	above 500,000 & upto 1,500,000
Service Enterprises – Investment in Equipments			

From: www.msme.gov.in

Little and Medium Enterprises (SMEs) assume a crucial job for the development of Indian economy by contributing 45% of modern yield, 40% of fares, utilizing 60 million individuals, make 1.3 million employments consistently and produce in excess of 8000 quality items for the Indian and global markets. SME's Contribution towards GDP in 2011 was 17% which is required to increment to 22% by 2012. There are around 30 million MSME Units in India and 12 million people are relied upon to join the workforce in the following 3 years.

SMEs are presently presented to more prominent open doors than at any other time for extension and expansion over the divisions. Indian market is developing quickly and Indian business visionaries are gaining astounding ground in different Industries like Manufacturing, Precision Engineering Design, Food Processing, Pharmaceutical, Textile and Garments, Retail, IT and ITES, Agro and Service segment.

Regardless of its estimable commitment to the Nation's economy, SME Sector does not get the required help from the concerned Government Departments, Banks, Financial Institutions and Corporate, which is an impediment in ending up progressively aggressive in the National and International Markets.

1.3   SMEs faces various issues

SMEs faces various issues - nonappearance of sufficient and auspicious saving money account, restricted capital and information, non-accessibility of reasonable innovation, low creation limit, insufficient promoting methodology, distinguishing proof of new markets, requirements on modernization and extensions, non-accessibility of very gifted work at moderate expense, catch up with different government organizations to determine issues and so forth.

There has been extensive enhancement in the business condition in the post-progression stage, however there is as yet far to go. We should make the virtual world the stage for working together notwithstanding when we are collaborating with approach producers.

The exchanges expenses of doing exchange India are somewhat high between 7-12% of the FOB estimation of fares and this is fairly high by worldwide measures. Additionally, we should be progressively aggressive and redesign our innovation just as abilities so the business issue can likewise be viably handled.

SMEs and the development of Economy:-

The early endeavors in HRD concentrated more on elevating practices intended to convey firm techniques and were fundamentally tending to the connection between worker conduct and friends procedure. In any case, firms have now moved towards concentrating more on preparing viewpoint and creative aptitudes for staying aggressive in the market, recommending the way that as the focused conditions change, firms assess their methodologies to fortify their present and future positions. The expanded challenge has changed the measures for embracing future HRD systems and the key changes lay essentially on:

1. Determination and work investigation
2. Prior arranging of work puts and enlisting approaches
3. Selection systems
4. Direction and refreshed training of new representatives
5. Evaluation of the pre and post productivity/yield
6. Demand driven information assimilation
7. Retaining of workers through motivating forces and advantages
8. Effective relational abilities with workers
9. Education and limit working of existing and new representatives
10. Loyalty and commitment of the workers

The proprietors of the SMEs dependably aim for proficient and sorted out big business which accomplishes high appraising as far as benefits yet not really compliments the representatives with abnormal state of inspiration under the ongoing topics in the executives factors, for example, reward and inspiration designs, procurement of new innovation and ability improvement are foundations for understanding the firm destinations. Furthermore, the recently made estimation of scholarly capital/resources, abilities, inventiveness, and data give an edge to company's aggressiveness in the market. This century will concentrate more on human component, since nature of representatives has been perceived as the most essential instrument for the long haul manageability of an undertaking.

The interest for the multifaceted ability is progressively seen as a zone of enthusiasm for open approach analysts and specialists. Home developed research in pulling in and overseeing ability is critical as SMEs especially in creating nations need capacities and framework to benefit as much as possible from their human abilities and as a result will in general have lower dimensions of normal profitability of work.

Notwithstanding long lasting adapting needs, preparing of people working in firms is a genuine requirement for any developing industry. In the South Asian SME area, considers, for example, feeble house preparing, absence of in-house abilities for formalized learning, restricted information about outer preparing openings, want for momentary outcomes, spending imperatives, predetermined number of students, and nonattendance of nearby companion bunches are perceived as the primary impediments.

Over the South Asian Association for Regional Cooperation (SAARC) district, human asset base still needs a great deal of expansion and specialized and money related help from the two governments and outside improvement accomplices. The human advancement list has been slacking on the lower side and needs further enhancement as expertise improvement and by and large information base.

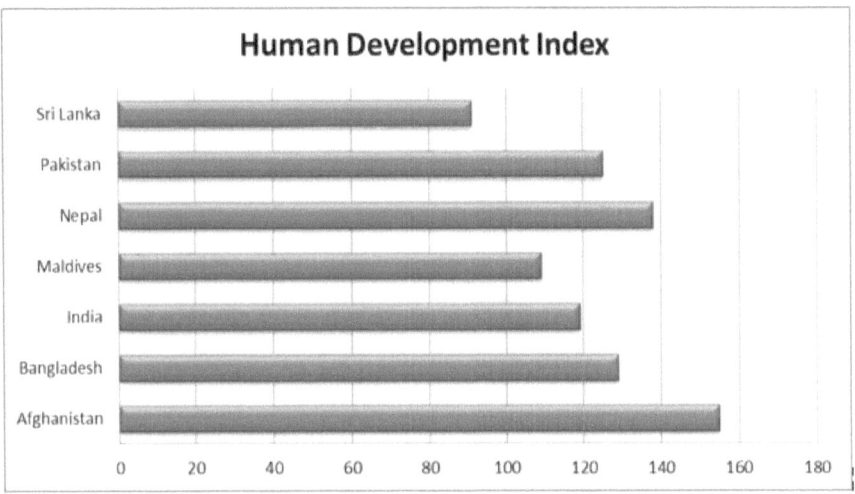

Figure: Human Development Index 2010

The little and medium undertakings today comprise an imperative portion of the Indian economy. The improvement of this division came about essentially because of the vision of our late Prime Minister Jawaharlal Nehru who looked to create center industry and have a supporting segment as little scale ventures. SMEs part has risen as a dynamic and lively area of the economy. Today, it represents about 35% of the gross estimation of yield in the assembling division and over 40% of the all out fares from the nation. As far as esteem included this segment represents about 40% of the esteem included the assembling segment. The area's commitment to work is second most noteworthy besides farming. The SMEs part has become quickly throughout the years. The development rates amid the different arrangement time frames have been noteworthy. The quantity of little scale units has expanded from an expected 6.79 million units in the year 1990-91 to more than 13 million in the year 2007-08. At the point when the execution of this division is seen against the development in the assembling and the business segment all in all, it ingrains trust in the flexibility of the SMEs part.

The Small and Medium Enterprises (SMEs) assume a reactant job in the improvement procedure of most economies as they establish a noteworthy piece of the mechanical action in these economies. This is reflected as their expanding number and rising extent in the general item fabricating, business, specialized developments and advancement of innovative abilities.

The commitment of SMEs in the improvement of Indian economy has been huge, both as far as commitment to GDP and production of business openings. They contribute around 20% of GDP and are the biggest generator of business (roughly 25 million). In India, SME part is the second biggest manager, after agribusiness. With the Indian economy developing at more than 9 percent and size of the economy crossing the $1 trillion imprint, the need of SMEs to raise capital is ending up progressively basic.

Little and Medium Enterprises assume an indispensable job for the development of Indian economy by contributing 45% of the mechanical yield, 40% of fares, 42 million in business, make one million employments consistently and creates in excess of 8000 quality items for the Indian and universal markets. Therefore, SMEs are today presented to more prominent open doors for development and enhancement over the areas.

The Indian market is developing quickly and Indian industry is gaining amazing ground in different Industries like Manufacturing, Precision Engineering, Food Processing, Pharmaceuticals, Textile and Garments, Retail, IT, Agro and Service segments. SMEs are finding expanding chances to upgrade their business exercises in center parts.

Raising the Profile of HR

SME authors frequently disregard the vital side of the HR and for the most part see it as another 'managerial capacity' bearing no immediate effect on the business. In such situations, it turns out to be progressively trying for the HR to propose or start any association wide change. It has turned out to be basic for the HR supervisors to break this form and raise their profile to wind up to a greater extent a key accomplice who can show the immediate worth of HR activities on the business. In this time of innovative disturbance, there are a lot of chances accessible to the HR administrators, for an occasion, they can use on rich individuals related information which the business can use to watch different patterns (ex. following steady loss, expanding commitment and so on).

Keeping up the soul of pioneering society

Overflowing with goals, trusts and enormous potential, SMEs in their underlying days as a rule convey a culture which is fun, fiery, quick moving and 'pioneering' in nature. It is for the most part contained youthful colleagues who work very intimately with one another and interface with seniors and authors all the more oftentimes. Be that as it may, when the business begins developing and winds up develop, it will in general lose its unique innovative soul – groups turn out to be enormous and visit associations with seniors/originators transform into month to month gatherings. Such situations present the conceivable outcomes of individuals feeling less esteemed and less settled in the framework, clearing route for upsetting and possible steady loss. In spite of the fact that testing, HR can assume a critical job here and keep up the way of life by keeping everybody educated, included and locked in. HR can use on social stage to convey about the basic improvements in the association, share examples of overcoming adversity, and even tune in to representatives' complaints. Such endeavors will help keep everybody associated – particularly amid the preliminary occasions when workers feel separated.

Adjusting Qualities

Another essential test which HR directors face in SMEs is to guarantee that the estimations of the originators are lined up with that of bigger worker gathering. Misalignment regularly happens when individuals from outside bring distinctive arrangement of qualities which remain in direct clash with that of authors and both the gatherings are sufficiently unbending to unlearn and grasp what is best for the venture. In such difficult circumstance, HR needs to assume a basic job by making mindfulness among leaders about the requirement for change. Two-way and straightforward correspondence between both the gatherings can cross over any barrier.

The significance of HR work in adding to the development of SMEs can't be denied. Be that as it may, it is as yet managing certain difficulties which can't be overlooked. While SMEs proceed with their development direction, the need is to perceive and address these difficulties so both SMEs and HR can cooperate to execute different attractive changes in the undertaking.

1.4   Job SME and Indian Economy

Little and medium measured ventures assume a focal job in the Indian economy. They are a noteworthy wellspring of enterprising abilities, advancement and work. SME organizations are the greatest supporter of the economy of any nation and the equivalent runs with Indian economy. Truth be told, SME is a standout amongst the most vital parts of Indian economy to the extent the quantity of jobs created from this portion. As over 65% of Indian populace lives in country and semi provincial territories, private company turns into a noteworthy wellspring of pay for some dwelling in these zones. After agribusiness, private venture in India is the second biggest manager of HR.

1.5 Fare Goals

The Fare Goals of SSI items have been recognized for 16 item gatherings.

The open doors in the little scale part are huge because of the accompanying variables:

1. Less Capital Concentrated
2. Extensive Advancement and Backing by Government
3. Reservation for Selective Production by little scale area
4. Project Profiles
5. Funding - Account and Endowments
6. Machinery Acquirement
7. Raw Material Acquirement
8. Manpower Preparing
9. Technical and Administrative abilities
10. Tooling and Testing support
11. Reservation for Select Buy by Government
12. Export Advancement
13. Growth popular in the residential market measure because of by and large financial development
14. Increasing Fare Potential for Indian items
15. Growth in Prerequisites for subordinate units because of the expansion in number of Greenfield units coming up in the substantial scale part. Little industry division has performed exceedingly well and empowered our nation to accomplish a wide proportion of mechanical development and broadening.

Work

SSI Area in India makes biggest business open doors for the Indian masses, next just to Farming. It has been evaluated that 100,000 rupees of interest in settled resources in the little scale area produces work for four people.

Insights from Ministry of Micro, Small and Medium Enterprises likewise mirror the development direction of SSI industry in India. The quantity of SSI units has expanded from 6.79 million out of 1990-91 to 13.37 million of every 2007-08 giving work to in excess of 32 million individuals in India.

Fare

SSI Division assumes a noteworthy job in India's present fare execution. 45%-half of the Indian Fares is contributed by SSI Division. Direct fares from the SSI Part represent almost 35% of absolute fares. Other than direct fares, it is evaluated that little scale modern units contribute around 15% to sends out in a roundabout way. This happens through trader exporters, exchanging houses and fare houses. They may likewise be as fare orders from substantial units or the creation of parts and segments for use for completed exportable merchandise.

It would astonish numerous to realize that non-customary items represent over 95% of the SSI sends out.

1. The fares from SSI division have been checking phenomenal development rates in this decade. It has been generally fuelled by the execution of pieces of clothing, cowhide and pearls and gems units from this division.
2. The item bunches where the SSI part rules in fares are sports merchandise, readymade pieces of clothing, woolen articles of clothing and knitwear, plastic items, handled nourishment and cowhide items. The SSI part is reorienting its fare system towards the new exchange routine being introduced by the WTO.

The Union Government has chosen to actualize a National Strategy for Manufacturing, drawn up by the National Manufacturing Competitiveness Council (NMCC), which will empower SMEs to accomplish intensity. The Strategy has recognized different need zones for activity viz., materials and articles of clothing, nourishment handling, IT equipment and hardware, calfskin and footwear, autos and auto-parts and synthetic concoctions and petrochemicals and pharma segments.

The Cluster Concept plainly is by all accounts India's response to worldwide challenge. A year ago the legislature had proposed to increment money related help to existing groups of Micro, Small and Medium Enterprises (MSME) up to as high as 80 percent of their monetary necessities under the eleventh Plan. This separated; the administration proposes to construct a pool of specialists under its National Manufacturing Competitiveness Program to empower MSMEs to end up aggressive. The advisors would be conveyed to a bunch of 8-10 organizations for around one year to eighteen months, with their expense being borne by the legislature.

In the attention on SMEs, the administration is bolstered by the United Nations Industrial Development Organization (UNIDO), which has proposed a five-year nation procedure for India. Group improvement is one fundamental piece of this methodology alongside projects went for updating mechanical capacity and building social capital in the nation's modern area. UNIDO is additionally investigating another trial of Twinning of Clusters as is found in the India-Italy Cluster Development Cooperation. Moreover, it is investigating new utilizations of Industrial bunch put together methodologies centering with respect to Corporate Social Responsibility and neediness easing in smaller scale undertakings.

The developing significance of Small and Medium Enterprises (SME) has been observed by the Planning Commission as well. Its agent administrator, Montek Singh Ahluwalia, said SME hold the way to the nation's modern advancement, at a capacity composed by the Indian Merchants Chamber (IMC) to perceive the determination of SMEs for the Ramkrishna Bajaj Award 2007.

It is interesting that an honor for SME was organized three years back and it is currently out of the blue that there is a beneficiary.

The very affirmation of this division demonstrates that the there is an unfolding of acknowledgment of the auxiliary changes that have occurred, said the agent director.

Obviously, SMEs have developed as a dynamic level of the economy as they have effectively assumed control as key supporters of the nation's GDP. Accurately hence, the Planning Commission is investigating the current arrangements and considering the vital changes required to make the SMEs job progressively proactive to help accomplish more prominent monetary objectives.

The Commission is of the firm supposition that in the radically changing financial situation, SMEs are what's to come. They are probably going to assume a significant job in prompt future, as they can cut out unit development show for the nation. The time has come to change corporate point of view and not to get influenced by budgetary highs

1.6 Socio-Economic Overview of the SAARC Region

Some key HRD markers in the SAARC Member States are given in Table 4.1. A portion of the part states performed feebly as far as training and wellbeing. By and large procedure of globalization has gotten new thoughts terms of preparing, innovation and cost minimization, which can possibly convert into riches gains. Enhanced HDI fabricates the certainty of remote financial specialists thusly bringing truly necessary thoughts and innovation for enhancing the information base. Low HRD has repercussions as low profitability, fall in fares, declining outside trade saves, and a generally wasteful use of assets.

HR benefits the foreign orientation of SMEs

HRD is a basic fixing to improve the profitability of SMEs. Created HR benefits the outside introduction of SMEs in the accompanying ways:

1. High quality HR pulls in Foreign Direct Investment (FDI) into the nation. The most recent and proficient innovation and skill are infused which prompts quick financial development.
2. Provision of better preparing or improvement of professional aptitudes to people may bring about expanding innovative action because of the imaginative procedure. The absence of imagination inability to imitate appropriate outside thoughts hampers firm improvement over the long haul.
3. A workforce having introduction with remote practices is very much aware of its rights and is better ready to secure against human rights and working environment infringement.
4. An internationally coordinated workforce acquires aggressive wages which at smaller scale level add to their prosperity and at large scale level aides in by and large destitution decrease.

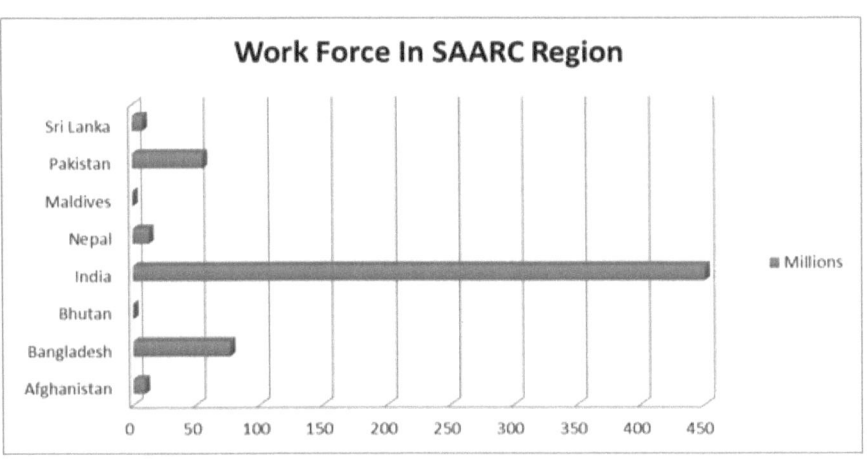

Figure: Work Force in SAARC Region

SAARC district is home to one of the biggest supply of human capital (Figure). The work drive investment rates in the SAARC area plainly recommend that Nepal and Bangladesh have most noteworthy support rates in the district and different nations are additionally not a long ways behind. A higher rate be that as it may, does not really suggest increasingly beneficial work compel. The past and current arrangements have been outfitted towards expanding the load of prepared work drive without understanding the ability advancement, imagination and development capacities of representatives which is an essential factor in deciding the long haul benefits in a period of worldwide challenge.

Sri Lanka	56.5	56.3	56.1	56	55.6	55.2	56.1	55	54.3
Pakistan	51.3	51.1	51	51.5	51.9	52.9	54	53.7	53.6
Nepal	70.4	70.6	70.6	70.7	70.8	70.9	71.1	71.2	71.5
Maldives	54.7	56.2	57.9	59.6	61.3	63.1	64.8	65.2	65.4
India	58.4	58.3	58.1	58	57.8	57.8	57.8	57.8	57.8
Bhutan	54.7	54.9	57.3	58.6	59.7	60.5	60.9	61	60.9
Bangladesh	70.6	70.7	70.8	70.9	70.9	70.9	70.8	70.7	70.6
Year	2000	2001	2002	2003	2004	2005	2006	2007	2008

SAARC Labor Force Participation Rates (%)

Table demonstrates the imperatives in the method for supported enhancement in HRD. In general South Asia's level of formal preparing is 17 percent which is less by any worldwide gauges. Nepal and Pakistan rank the most minimal. Sri Lanka has the most astounding extent of firms offering formal preparing. The normal number of lasting representatives has been more than the impermanent workers, subsequently proposing a solid requirement for in house HRD in the organizations. South Asian firms have immense potential and require solid preparing disposition towards its representatives to remain all around aggressive. The way that low level of firms distinguished work laws as a requirement is additionally intelligent of these elements staying little or now and again casual with the goal that they don't go under the ambit of work laws. Open arrangements must see SMEs graduating in to winding up substantial firms.

Countries	All Countries	South Asia	Afghanistan	Bangladesh	India	Nepal	Pakistan	Sri Lanka	Bhutan
Years			2008	2007	2006	2009	2007	2004	2009
Firms offering Formal Training (%)	34.3	16.8	14.5	16.1	15.9	8.7	6.7	32.5	23.2
Avg. Temporary Employees	7.8	13.3	17.6	18.1	1.6	2.6	11.5	33.1	8.7
Avg. Permanent Employees	49.2	93.5	20.7	162.4	34.2	13.2	32.4	367.9	23.5
Firms Identifying Labor Laws (%)	11.4	10.7	4.5	3.8	9.1	9.2	6.3	25.5	16.4

Table: Imperatives to HRD

Study demonstrates that India and Pakistan fallen behind Asian economies in the Total Factor Productivity (TFP) development amid 1981 to 2007. In any case, the all the more concerning viewpoint is that the hole between South Asia and rest of the rising Asian economies will increment further in future. The absolute Asian fares amid years 2005 to 2009 have expanded from $ 132 to $219 billion. In spite of the fact that the pattern is empowering however this development is coordinated by consistently developing challenge with different nations who are bringing most recent advancements, increasingly talented work drive, enhanced strategies of the board and other limit building programs for its representatives.

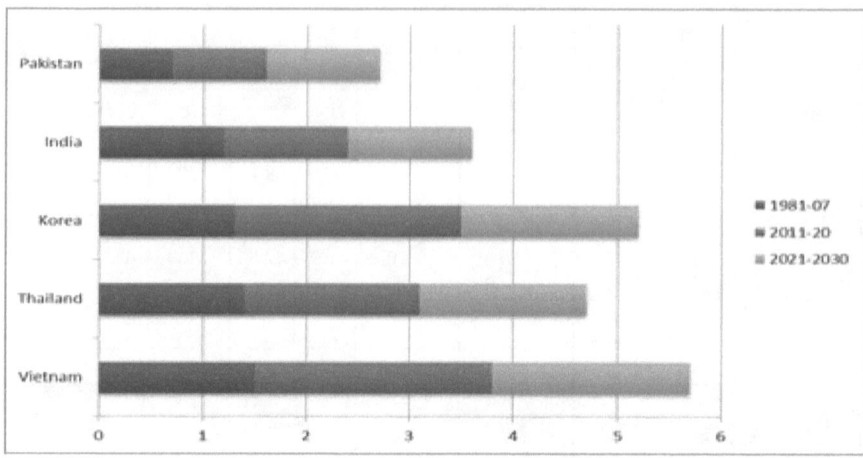

Figure: All out Factor Productivity over the South Asia

The hole between fares from South Asia and rest of the world (Figure) is still considerably huge and must be crossed over if astounding HR can help SMEs in accomplishing the ideal economies of scale.

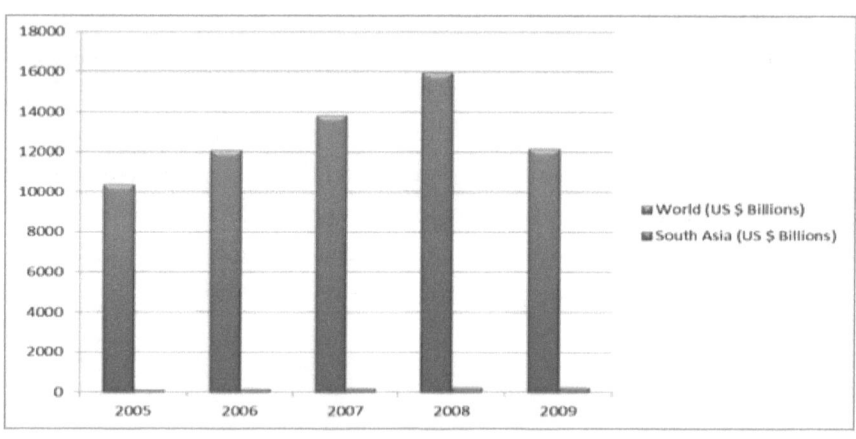

Figure: Fare Performance South Asia versus Rest of the World

The South Asian offer in worldwide fares is just 2 percent. The case of China and Korea in adjusting HRD forms with developing worldwide markets is likewise worth referencing.

1.7   Financial Overview of the SAARC Region

India experienced grim financial conditions in mid 1990s. Soviet Union in that period was the principle exchanging accomplice of India. The nation confronted gigantic parity of installment issues when Soviet Union was disintegrated. So as to moderate the circumstance, Indian government started the long haul exchange and speculation advancement plan. Remote direct speculations were invited, open restraining infrastructures were nullified, and keeping money, administrations, and tertiary parts were by and large created. Indian government organized the advancement of cash and capital market. Since the progression of business sectors in the mid-1990s, India has encountered good financial development. India is among the quickest developing economies of the world. Figure demonstrates the rising genuine GDP development rate of India from 1990 to 2007.

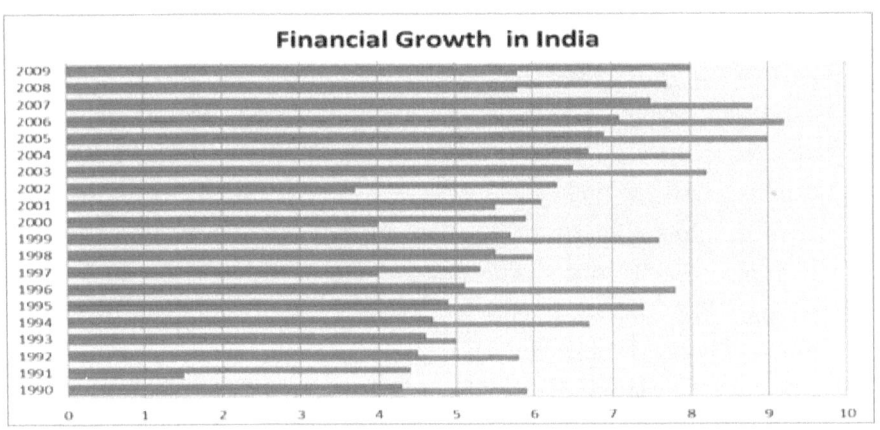

Figure: Financial Growth in India

Table demonstrates the financial circumstance of India. The esteem expansion by horticulture area as level of GDP was 17 percent in 2009. The real farming yields of the nation are wheat, rice, coarse grains, oilseeds, sugar, cotton, jute, and tea. Esteem expansion of mechanical division as level of GDP was 28 percent in 2009. The major mechanical yield of the nation are materials, prepared sustenance, steel, hardware, transport gear, concrete, aluminum, composts, mining, oil, synthetic concoctions, and PC programming. The real imports of the nation are oil, apparatus and transport hardware, electronic merchandise, eatable oils, manures, synthetic concoctions, gold, materials, iron and steel. U.S., China, U.A.E., EU, Russia, Japan are the significant exchanging accomplices of India. Indian economy has seen an ongoing blast in administrations segments which altogether contribute 56.3 percent of GDP.

1.8   Globalization's implications for HRD:-

For those working in a universal setting globalization presents HRD specialists with the chance to convey a wide scope of HRD intercessions that increase the value of an association. So as to accomplish this they have to work in association with key partners at both a vital and operational dimension. Dealing with these partner connections is a testing and complex errand and is affected by how the HRD work is organized. To be fruitful HRD experts must comprehend worldwide patterns and the issues that issue most to their partners. This information should be coordinated with a comprehension of the worldwide economy and distinctive national HRD arrangements and rehearses; and a comprehension of social contrasts and how these can affect on formal and casual working environment instructing. Furthermore HRD specialists must realize how to configuration, convey, and assess vital worldwide preparing in a global domain. This empowers the HRD capacity to plan mediations that are connected to the accomplishment of authoritative objectives. For business partnerships the vast majority of these objectives will be monetarily arranged.

HRD ought to receive an influential position to guarantee globalization conveys advantages to mankind. In a comparable contend for 'socially Cognizant's HRD which includes advancing moral and socially dependable administration and authority. These thoughts reflect two things: first, the developing impact on associations of business morals and corporate social duty (CSR), the impact of a humanist point of view on learning and HRD, which is talked about in the following section. The issue for some HRD professionals is that a position of authority remains a goal as opposed to a reality.

The nature and motivation behind HRD at a hierarchical dimension contrasts crosswise over nations and areas and between various kinds of association. There are instances of advanced indigenous ways to deal with HRD in the creating economies of India and China, in spite of the fact that preparation costs are limited in the Chinese assembling division. Outside direct speculation (FDI) organizations put resources into HRD more than indigenous organizations and this is helping in the exchange of HRD rehearses among creating and creating economies. This pattern isn't confined to Western multinationals. For example, the Korean vehicle maker Hyundai has connected its very own portion HRM arrangements in India, especially preparing projects which have been intended to fortify worker faithfulness to the organization.

Maybe the best test confronting HRD specialists working in a universal limit is the means by which to work successfully at both a worldwide and a neighborhood level to be able to think all around however act locally. This is imperative since it has been progressively perceived that nation and neighborhood setting impact the HR practices of multinationals. A topical case of this is the requirement for HRD experts in multinationals to have 'a far reaching comprehension of the social' whenever Westernized HRD rehearses are to be adjusted viably to the earth. Albeit numerous littler associations presently working in the worldwide commercial center tend not to utilize pro HRM or HRD specialists there is as yet a requirement for administrators to think thusly. The HRD mediations are arranged as 'formal intercessions' and 'casual exercises' with both requiring cooperation between HRD specialists and senior/line chiefs to varying degrees relying upon the authoritative setting. In spite of the fact that these necessities are one-sided to multinationals, many influence different kinds of association to a lesser or more noteworthy degree. For example, non-benefit associations working in a few nations or areas and going after financing need senior supervisors to have compelling worldwide administration abilities; and, all associations working in worldwide markets, from private venture to multinationals, need to comprehend about change the executives. Formal mediations and exercises have been arranged as preparing and improvement, profession advancement or authoritative advancement. Seemingly, all casual exercises are types of hierarchical improvement which rely upon a blend of help and training abilities by HRD specialists and line chiefs.

1.9   Kind of Labor in SME:-

Capital power is the term in financial aspects for the measure of settled or genuine capital present in connection to different elements of creation, particularly work. At the dimension of either a generation procedure or the total economy, it might be assessed by the capital/work proportion, for example, from the focuses along a capital/work isoquant. This is the place methods are utilized to create that utilization moderately more capital than work. Numerous businesses are currently similar to this including the vehicle and steel enterprises.

Capital-concentrated ventures utilize an extensive segment of funding to purchase costly machines, contrasted with their work costs. The term came to fruition in the mid-to late-nineteenth-century as production lines, for example, steel or iron jumped up around the recently industrialized world. With the additional cost of hardware, there was more prominent monetary hazard. This makes new capital-concentrated manufacturing plants with cutting edge apparatus a little offer of the commercial center, despite the fact that they raise efficiency and yield. A few organizations normally thought to be capital-serious are railroads, carriers, oil creation and refining, broadcast communications, mining, substance plants, electric power plants, and so forth.

A business is capital serious on the off chance that it requires substantial capital interest in purchasing resources in respect to the dimension of offers or benefits that those advantages can produce. Capital concentrated business will commonly have some blend of the high deterioration costs, high boundaries to passage and a lot of settled resources on the accounting report.

Only a capital escalated business may endeavor to lessen operational adapting by, for instance, renting or leasing resources, a work concentrated one may attempt to decrease operational equipping by redistributing or computerization.

Capital Intensive Industry alludes to that industry, which requires generous measure of capital for the creation of products. In the Capital Serious Businesses extent of capital included is a lot higher than the extent of work. This is on the grounds that the mechanical structure and industry type require high esteem interests in capital Resources. For the most part, the capital serious ventures create abnormal state of benefit. The vast measure of capital put resources into these ventures produce high rate of return and this thus prompts progressively capital speculation.

Capital concentrated businesses include abnormal state of settled expense. Thus they include higher level of hazard. On the off chance that the business volume decays, benefits earned by the business experience a sharp decline as the settled cost part can't be expelled or diminished. Along these lines, in the event that advertise request decays, at that point the capital serious enterprises experience the ill effects of more misfortune contrasted with the work concentrated businesses.

Car industry, concoction industry and oil refinery industry are fundamentally capital escalated ventures, which require extensive capital speculation for beginning up the business and to maintain the business too. Because of the way that all capital serious businesses require extensive volume of monetary assets for gazing up, the quantity of new participants to any capital escalated industry is generally less contrasted with any work concentrated industry.

The advantage of capital concentrated industry is that it guarantees abnormal state of profitability. This is conceivable in light of the fact that, the capital speculations are utilized to outfit the business with fundamental devices and cutting edge apparatus and this utilization of trend setting innovation raises the efficiency of work bringing about more noteworthy yield. As the capital force of capital concentrated businesses result in more elevated amount of efficiency, these enterprises have the ability to create more salary and along these lines more benefit. Along these lines, in long run, the capital concentrated enterprises can give a higher expectation for everyday comforts to any economy.

The level of capital force is anything but difficult to quantify in ostensible terms. It is just the proportion of the complete cash estimation of capital gear to the all out potential yield. Be that as it may, this measure need not be identified with genuine financial movement since it can ascend because of swelling. At that point the inquiry emerges, how would we measure the "genuine" measure of capital merchandise? Do we use book esteem (authentic cost)? Or on the other hand substitution cost? Or on the other hand the cost advocated by the present limited estimation of future benefits? Or then again do we essentially "empty" the absolute current cash estimation of capital hardware by the normal cost of capital merchandise?

When this issue has been fathomed, the capital contention raises its appalling head. This contention calls attention to that proportion of capital power isn't free of the circulation of salary, with the goal that adjustments in the proportion of benefits to compensation lead to changes in estimated capital force.

'Capital' alludes to the hardware, apparatus, vehicles, etc. that a business uses to make its item or administration. Capital-escalated forms are those that require a moderately abnormal state of capital venture contrasted with the work cost. These procedures are bound to be profoundly computerized and to be utilized to create on a huge scale. Capital-escalated generation is bound to be related with stream creation (see underneath) however any sort of generation may require costly hardware.

Capital is a long haul venture for most organizations, and the expenses of financing, keeping up and deteriorating this hardware speak to a significant overhead. So as to augment effectiveness, firms need their capital venture to be completely used (see notes on limit usage). In a capital-escalated procedure, it very well may be exorbitant and tedious to increment or abatement the size of creation.

A work serious business is one in which the fundamental expense is that of work, and it is high contrasted with deals or esteem included. Work escalated creation techniques include significant work input and are regularly utilized in labor copious economies. In labor serious generation forms, cost of work is similarly lower than expense of capital. Agribusiness, mining, angling, inns, and eateries are work concentrated exercises. Tis are the place the extent of work utilized in delivering the item is generally high. Work will more often than not be utilized rather than capital.

Labor Intensive Industry alludes to that industry, which requires considerable measure of human work to create the modern items. As the name recommends, these work serious businesses use work seriously. This implies, the extent in which work is utilized for generation is a lot higher than the extent of capital.

In these work serious ventures, work costs are significantly more critical than the capital expenses.

1. Work serious ventures generally don't convey high settled expense. In actuality, higher level of variable expenses is acquired in the work concentrated ventures.
2. As these businesses don't include abnormal state of settled expense or abnormal state of support cost, they hold high winning potential. Be that as it may, if there should arise an occurrence of abnormal state of expansion in the Economy, the work concentrated industry can endure to some degree.
3. This is on the grounds that, in the seasons of abnormal state of swelling, the workers can uncover their reluctance to work at a similar dimension of pay, as expansion brings down their genuine profit.

Hospitality industry and coal mining industry are the enterprises, which hold a work escalated industry structure. For the immature and creating economies, work concentrated industry structure can be turned out to be a superior alternative than a capital serious one. The nations, which are not rich and create low dimension of pay, Labor escalated industry can bring monetary development and thriving. In a large portion of the cases, these low pay nations experience the ill effects of shortage of capital yet are honored with plentiful work constrain. On the off chance that they can utilize this inexhaustible work constrain appropriately in their industry creation, at that point they can encounter mechanical development. Supply of superbly gifted work to any industry can trigger the business development rate. Along these lines, the immature nations can enhance their mechanical economy without doing overwhelming capital speculation.

In addition, exportation of the items made by work escalated businesses can fortify the fare base of any creating Nation. These fares help the economies in:-

1. Winning outside trade
2. This can be utilized for bringing in basic merchandise and ventures.
3. As the work escalated enterprises produce work on an expansive scale, they in a path add to monetary prosperity.

In less created economies work bounty is an inalienable trademark. All things considered, work concentrated businesses and work escalated assembling forms are normal. As a rule terms, work concentrated businesses require more prominent amount of physical or human exertion in their assembling procedure. Cowhide preparing, piece of clothing producing, farming based businesses like tea handling, and flavors fabricating are average instances of work serious optional financial exercises. Managing an account, accommodation, and ITES (data innovation empowered administrations) are work serious monetary exercises in tertiary or administrations sector Advantages of work escalated procedures

For any assembling procedure, cost of capital is accepted to remain to some degree consistent and work cost as a most prevalent variable. Creation cost is all the more effectively controlled in labor serious procedures since work size can be changed relying upon interest variances of market.

For less created economies, where work is accessible in plenitude it is useful to utilize work serious strategies for generation not exclusively to utilize accessible assets yet additionally to keep creation costs down. Accessibility of shabby work is a typical wonder in labor surplus economies. Direction of utilized work is most advantageous method for controlling creation cost in short run.

'Work' alludes to the general population required to complete a procedure in a business. Work serious procedures are those that require a moderately abnormal state of work contrasted with capital venture. These procedures are bound to be utilized to deliver individual or customized items, or to create on a little scale. The expenses of work are: compensation and different advantages, enrollment, preparing, etc.

Some adaptability in limit might be accessible by utilization of additional time and transitory staff, or by laying-off laborers. Long haul development relies upon having the capacity to select adequate appropriate staff. Work concentrated procedures are bound to be found in Job generation and in littler scale ventures.

Work escalated alludes to the blends of factor contributions for a firm. On the off chance that a firm creates a decent that is work escalated it implies that the quantity of units of work is high in respect to the number units of capital (or whatever other factor of generation there is). For instance, instruction and instructing is extremely work concentrated, as the showing field needs many individuals to teach and deal with the organization of training. It is additionally not likely that the encouraging division won't move to ever be capital serious.

Any firm that creates a decent that is concentrated in any factor is powerless against stuns or changes in the expense of that factor. In the event that the cost of work expands it will extraordinarily ruin the capacity the company's capacity to create that great.

All in all, the 'experts' of Labor-serious exercises are:

1. Adaptability (people are more adaptable and versatile than machines), and
2. Minimization of direct front capital venture (machines cost a ton).

The 'cons' of Labor-concentrated exercises are:

1. High per-unit generation costs under high-volume creation
2. Changeability in yield quality (machines do dreary assignment the very same way inevitably, and people don't)

3. Poor versatility (a machine can put out a ton of gadgets, people not really).

There is nothing about "Work Intensive" actives that is either naturally great or innately awful. In the event that you live in a financially all around created nation (like the UK in 2011), at that point unit work costs are high and along these lines a "Work Intensive" undertaking is probably going to be costly. In the event that you live in a not really very much created nation, at that point unit work expenses would be low, and a "Work Intensive" undertaking will be economical.

For instance, in the event that you take a gander at amazing structures in London that were worked before the year 1900, you will see that there are numerous lovely compositional subtleties, for example, hand-made trim and moldings. Work was shabby, so Labor-concentrated occupations were ample. On the off chance that you take a gander at structures after the year 2000, you will see few work escalated subtleties since they are excessively costly.

The strategy that an organization utilizes relies upon a few things:-

A) Size of the organization - little organizations is regularly not in a situation to bear the cost of costly capital gear. Regardless of whether they might they be able to are frequently not ready to utilize it enough to legitimize the expense.

B) The cost of the variables of generation - despite the fact that a machine might be accessible to carry out the responsibility, it may not be advantageous if the measure of work required costs less. Firms along these lines take a gander at the expense of work and capital before choosing the amount to utilize.

C) The item - a few items loan themselves better to being created by capital than others. Mass-created regular things are unquestionably bound to be delivered in a capital-escalated way, though administrations and items with an increasingly singular inclination are bound to be created utilizing a huge extent of work.

There is an issue of picking between work concentrated enterprises or Labor serious techniques and Capital Intensive businesses or Capital Intensive Methods. In immature nations, because of ceaseless joblessness or shabby work to capital is favored.

The most proficient utilization of assets in less created nations will in general support work concentrated strategies. For advancements, it would likewise pursue the Capital Saving and Labor utilizing developments, it would be favored. It is gainful to receive capital-escalated systems to expand profitability.

Work constrain is a pivotal idea utilized by Karl Marx in his scrutinize of industrialist political economy. He viewed work control as the most essential of the profitable powers of individuals. Work power can be basically characterized as work-limit, the capacity to do work. Work control exists in any sort of society, yet on what terms it is exchanged or joined with methods for creation to deliver products and ventures has generally changed significantly. Under free enterprise, as per Marx, the beneficial forces of work show up as the innovative intensity of capital. To be sure "work control at work" turns into a segment of capital, it works as working capital. Work turns out to be simply work, specialists turn into a conceptual work drive, and the authority over work turns out to be for the most part an administration privilege.

"By work power or limit with respect to work is to be comprehended the total of those psychological and physical capacities existing in an individual, which he practices at whatever point he creates an utilization estimation of any portrayal." Or "Work control, be that as it may, turns into a reality just by its activity; it sets itself in real life just by working. Yet, in this manner a positive amount of human muscle, nerve. Cerebrum, &c., is squandered, and these require to be reestablished."

There is an unmistakable refinement among work and work

control. "Work" alludes to the real action or exertion of delivering merchandise or administrations. Here and there alludes as "work administrations." On the other hand, "work control" (or "laboring force") alludes to an individual's capacity to work, his or her muscle-power, aptitude and intellectual prowess.

1.10   Current Economy and Human Capital:-

We use book generation per capita as a pointer of human capital, so as to examine two issues:

(1) Does human capital increment welfare development in the early present day time frame?
(2) Was there contingent assembly in pre mechanical, when we control for human capital and different factors?

We locate a positive response to the two inquiries. This is very astonishing: A persuasive paper had contended that human capital (estimated as evaluated education) had no vital effect amid the early current time frame. Additionally as far as unite/veer, the basic insight was that welfare patterns were wandering (albeit unequivocally as opposed to restrictively).

We characterize welfare development as the development of genuine wages, in light of the fact that those speak to a marker of welfare that can be estimated pretty much precisely for the fifteenth to nineteenth century in various nations. Human capital is extensively characterized, containing parts, for example, education, numeracy, the load of thoughts that can be put away and recovered and different segments.

Human capital is the supply of skills, information and identity traits exemplified in the capacity to perform work in order to create monetary esteem. It is the characteristics picked up by a specialist through instruction and experience. Numerous early monetary speculations allude to it basically as workforce, one of three elements of generation, and view it as a fungible asset homogeneous and effectively exchangeable. Different originations of this work abstain from these suspicions.

Contrasted with the disciplinary load of financial aspects, with its foundations in established political economy of the eighteenth and nineteenth hundreds of years, HRM falls into the classification of little broil. It was set up in the USA as a scholarly order amid the mid-1980s is as yet hunting down a hypothetical system (single or numerous) to loan thoroughness to a quickly developing collection of experimental research. Be that as it may, while HRM researchers have generally built up their methodology separate to the control of financial matters, since the mid-1980s market analysts have turned their eyes to issues tended to inside HRM. Our contention here is this to a great extent uneven incorporation has not been productive since (an) a large number of the scientific apparatuses from the financial experts' secret stash are wrong to comprehend the administration of work and (b) with some outstanding special cases.

As indicated by the significance of human capital in monetary development, many creating nations have endeavored to improve human capital aggregation in their own nations with various styles and particularly open help. These endeavors are being uncovered to be seen effectively in these nations expanded the normal long stretches of training. In such conditions which had demonstrated a solid positive connection between per capita pay and physical capital amassing, numerous examinations are viewed as the inquiry, could influence expanding human capital on development advancement in these nations? As such is that, is the causal connection between human capital and monetary development single direction relationship of financial development to human capital? Have considered these nations human capital as an extravagance and shopper merchandise? Hardly any examinations about the recurrence of nations with concentrated normal assets particularly raw petroleum demonstrates that for the most part the connection between human capital and monetary development has been the relationship of one-sided financial development to human capital and human capital is generally devoured item in short and medium term because of lease center assets and lease state conduct and Dutch ailment marvels and outcomes coming about because of it in the field of modern arrangement and political economy in such nations.

Contemporary investigation recognizes substantial, physical, or nonhuman capital merchandise from different types of capital, for example, human capital. Human capital is epitomized in a person and is gained through instruction and preparing, regardless of whether formal or at work. Human capital is essential in present day financial hypothesis. Training is a key component in clarifying financial development after some time.

Four sorts of settled capital (which is depicted as that which deals with a pay or advantage without revolving around or advancing pros). The four sorts were:-

1. Useful machines, *instruments* of the exchange;
2. Buildings as the methods for getting income;
3. Improvements of land;
4. The gained and valuable capacities of the considerable number of occupants or individuals from the general public.

"Fourthly, of the got and important limits of the extensive number of tenants or people from the overall population. The getting of such capacities, by the upkeep of the acquirer in the midst of his preparation, study, or apprenticeship, constantly costs a veritable cost, which is a capital settled and recognized, allegorically, in his person. Those abilities, as they make a piece of his fortune, so do they in like manner that of the general public to which he has a place. The enhanced expertise of a laborer might be considered in indistinguishable light from a machine or instrument of exchange which encourages and compresses work, and which, however it costs a specific cost, reimburses that cost with a benefit.".

In this way, the beneficial intensity of work are both reliant on the division of work. "The best enhancement in the gainful forces of work, and most of the expertise, adroitness, and judgment with which it is anyplace coordinated, or connected, appear to have been the impacts of the division of work". There is a mind boggling connection between the division of work and human capital.

Human capital is an impalpable resource as it isn't claimed by the firm that utilizes it. Fundamentally, human capital lands at 9am and leaves at 5pm. Human capital when seen from a period point of view expends time in one of key exercises:-

1. Knowledge (exercises including one representative),
2. Collaboration (exercises including more than 1 representative),
3. Processes (exercises explicitly centered around the learning and cooperative exercises produced by authoritative structure -, for example, storehouse impacts, inward legislative issues, and so on.) and
4. Absence (yearly leave, wiped out leave, occasions, and so forth.).

At the point when human capital is evaluated by movement based costing by means of time assignments it ends up conceivable to survey human capital hazard. Human capital hazard happens when the association works underneath feasible operational greatness levels. For instance, if a firm could sensibly decrease blunders and revamp (the Process part of human capital) from 10,000 hours for every annum to 2,000 hours with achievable innovation, the distinction of 8,000 hours is human capital hazard. At the point when wage costs are connected to this distinction (the 8,000 hours) it ends up conceivable to monetarily esteem human capital hazard inside an authoritative viewpoint.

Human capital peril accumulates in four basic classes:-

1. Absence (exercises identified with representatives not appearing for work, for example, wiped out leave, mechanical activity, and so on.). Unavoidable nonappearance is alluded to as Statutory Absence. Every single other classes of nonappearance are named "Controllable Absence";
2. Collaborative exercises are identified with the consumption of time between more than one worker inside a hierarchical setting. Models include: gatherings, telephone calls, teacher drove preparing, and so on.
3. Knowledge Activities are identified with time consumptions by a solitary individual and incorporate finding/recovering data, inquire about, email, informing, blogging, data investigation, and so forth.;
4. Process exercises are learning and community oriented exercises that outcome because of hierarchical setting, for example, mistakes/revise, manual information change, stress, legislative issues, and so on.

1.11 HRM in SME:-

The SMEs that fundamentally assess their business condition and look to comprehend their industry and focused conditions will in general embrace the most appropriate arrangement of HRD rehearses. The SMEs that consider the focused circumstance and human asset methodology at the same time endure the trial of time better.

The achievement of a firm relies upon its short and long haul destinations that go for advancing a culture of learning in a coordinated authoritative structure, cutting-edge innovation, high caliber of data sources and all the more essentially a human asset that reacts to association's objectives. Thinking about this, HRD is essential for company's more extended run key improvement.

All together for the workers to complete their jobs and capacities in overseeing effectively, they should be all around prepared and taught to assume multifaceted job. Preparing can be an incredible main thrust for firm extension and building up its capacities. The impact of preparing towards big business development, affirmed that SMEs that expansion the preparation exertion, figured out how to expand its development in term of offers and incomes. Aptitudes required for overhauling exercises among the best administration of the organizations lead to an enhancement of the efficiency level and consumer loyalties.

The job of preparing in an association for enhancing productivity and information has been compelling for the SME improvement. The preparation angle has noteworthy commitment towards firm advancement and there is critical enhancement still required towards expanding the supply of numerous abilities which thus can convey complex focal points to the working structure of the firm and all the more significantly affecting the execution of the firm over the long haul.

The quickly developing economies and the ones with aggressive abilities have understood the significance of HRD as of earlier significance and subsequently put vigorously in HR as limit building and obtaining of current aptitudes.

India over the most recent two decades has indicated striking development in the administrations part. The financial progression has brought mechanical change and furthermore craving for expanded challenge. Understanding this IT industry has appeared and has copied the accepted procedures of HR and this thus has affected the fares decidedly. The information was assembled utilizing nitty gritty polls and Vans COM Database 1993-2002. The inventive enrollment and pay rehearses have affected the firm execution emphatically.

India has been at the cutting edge as far as expanded fares

volume and esteem. This is trailed by Pakistan and Bangladesh. Anyway the hole among India and other SAARC economies is required to stay vast except if generous vertical and flat incorporation happens among these nations. There stays abundant open door for expanding the fares base by means of SME improvement and further putting resources into HRD through the arrangement of refreshed preparing and new innovation use. Right now the SMEs contribute 40 percent to the fares of India with yield commitment of 45 percent in the business. It delivers in excess of 8000 items and utilizes in excess of 60 million individuals. The expanded administrations segment commitment in Indian economy has took into consideration progressing of SME area on an increasingly practical premise.

Indian car industry as becoming sought after and is along these lines proper arrangements for HRD are required for building up this sub part. Vehicle auxiliary firms are similarly essential and ought to be made piece of the formal part however much as could reasonably be expected. Eight basic components are recognized to be of most extreme significance, of which HRD at the lower level of representatives is the key factor for creating future interior and outside economies of scale. Most preparing offices are just restricted to administrative dimension positions. Anyway it is notable that advancements can be invigorated by including the lower level in the imaginative procedure.

In India an extensive number of firms are proprietor controlled privately-owned companies. Anyway worldwide changes are constraining Indian firms to change customary methodology and move towards giving workers a stake in business. The beginning stage is to give them the vital life and work abilities, with the goal that they can practice most extreme open door for development.

In the quickly changing situation of HRD rehearses, India has reclassified its job through joining of new strategies for expertise improvement. This extents from enhanced administration conveyance, limit fabricating, and presenting effective practices in the commercial center. The preparation needs that are connected with the progressions occurring in the business strategies territorially and internationally.

The Indian SMEs Vision 2020 blueprints the significance of SME improvement concentrating on the part of "progress" as the main perpetual thing. The procedure of progress has quickened as of late because of macroeconomic change occurring both locally and all around.

In a period of borderless and market-situated economy, the two major worldwide monetary powers which are viewing for world consideration are:

(a) The rise of 'another economy' supported by data and correspondence innovations and

(b) Developing shakiness and vulnerability connected to outer stuns. The Vision 2020 features that the consideration ought to be occupied towards propelling the workers who would then be able to create and exchange, quality innovative items over universal limits. The Vision involves three parts: best in class preparing, advancement of development and enhanced proficiency.

The established financial experts like Adam Smith viewed HRD as an asset for the abundance of countries. The advanced challenge is based the preparation which thusly relies upon the economic situations, association's own exhibitions, business attributes, administrative initiative and the dimension of social capital.

The SMEs in India require help from the general population segment regarding fundamental commercial center challenge changes, access to back, innovation, calculated help, HRD and business enterprise advancement. Current HRD ought to be embraced in a way that guarantees advantages of globalization to laborers on an even premise. HRD which has includes advancing moral and socially dependable administration and initiative. These thoughts reflects two things: First, the developing impact on associations of business morals and Corporate Social Responsibility (CSR) and furthermore the impact of a humanist point of view in learning and HRD.

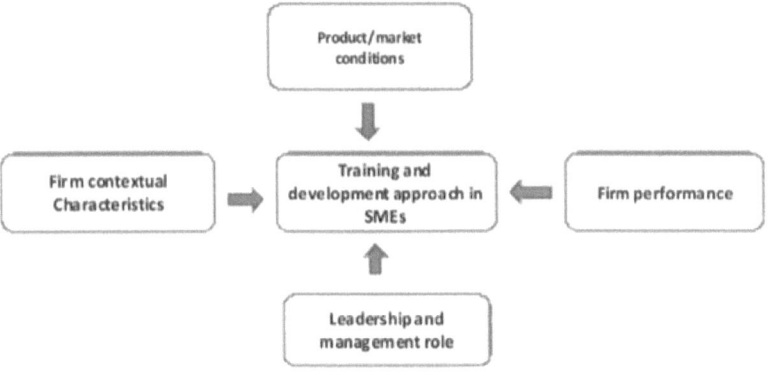

Figure: Present day Competition Model

The significance of strategy in the territories of instruction, work, expertise improvement, innovation and smaller scale fund has vital resonations on the HRD adequacy in the SMEs. It will be enlightening to have an elevated perspective on some of ongoing arrangements of SAARC nations for the inspire of the human asset. The greater part of the analysis beneath depends on distributed government sources crosswise over SAARC nations for the elevate of the human asset.

Instruction gives essential information and aptitudes required for continued development of the economy and by and large intelligent advancement. The significance of instruction is perceived, as the establishment obstruct for accomplishing national socio-targets and building a progressively comprehensive, evenhanded and maintainable society. SAARC has a statistic advantage with a huge youth populace. Be that as it may, this preferred standpoint must be acknowledged whether monetary open doors for youth develop a considerable scale. Instruction among different components can help in extending such chances.

The number of inhabitants in India is evaluated to be around 1140 million and huge segment of the populace is youthful. So as to guarantee the fair access to instruction for all nationals,

Indian government has coordinated the estimations of secularism, libertarianism, regard for equitable conventions and common freedoms and journey for equity in the standard training framework. It goes for making subjects furnished with important information, abilities and qualities to construct a comprehensive and dynamic culture. The Mission of Ministry of Human Resource Development and the Department of Higher Education is as per the following:

1. Provide more noteworthy chances of access to advanced education with value to all the qualified people and specifically to the powerless areas.
2. Expand access by supporting existing foundations, building up new establishments, supporting State Governments and Non-Government Organizations/common society to enhance open endeavors went for evacuating territorial or different awkward nature that exist at present.
3. Initiate approaches and projects for fortifying examination and advancements and support organizations open or private to participate in extending the boondocks of information.
4. Skilled advancement to receive the rewards of the statistic favorable position of the nation.
5. Promote the nature of advanced education by putting resources into framework and personnel, advancing scholastic changes, enhancing administration and institutional rebuilding.
6. Engage with common society, state governments and with the global network in promotion of information, language and culture.

The expanding consideration on human asset (HR) in little and medium endeavors (SMEs) is a relatively late marvel. HR-analysts have to a great extent overlooked the SMEs, despite the fact that littler organizations could be productive subjects for experimental examination in light of the fact that their numbers, the development rates and not least decent variety in the subjective parts of the board rehearses. Along these lines HR in SMEs has been a white spot on the guide, and this regardless of the trademark Danish mechanical structure, for example the expansive extent of SMEs; the long convention for a somewhat systematized and efficient work showcase, which could give a premise to an increasingly proficient way to deal with HR, lastly the alleged exceptionally great reason for future aggressiveness, because of the qualities describing representatives just as chiefs in Danish organizations, for example law based administration style, casual sorting out, adaptable working course of action and so on.

On the developing significance of Human Resource Management and Development for little and medium-sized endeavors (SMEs) in industrialized high development nations. All the more explicitly, it will accept the Indian circumstance as a case to show the connection between from one viewpoint major financial, innovative and social changes in the SMEs' surroundings and, on the other, the inclination to an increasingly vital reasoning on the administration of the HR of this kind of firms.

From a SME-point of view, the investigation of Human Resource Development (HRD) is applicable for a few reasons. To begin with, it is seen that SMEs consider their HR issues to have top need. Also, HR is of extraordinary enthusiasm to SMEs in light of the fact that for these organizations HR assume a crucial job in creating and continuing upper hand. In little firms this is much increasingly significant because of their particular work associations and in light of the fact that SMEs are moderately work concentrated. Additionally, as an immediate consequence of the little scale, every individual representative speaks to a substantive piece of the SMEs workforce, along these lines expanding the significance of each and every HR-choice.

The point of this examination on HRD in SMEs is to investigate if and to what degree the particular qualities of little and medium undertakings (SMEs) lead to the need of explicit HR systems. We will edify this issue by investigating SMEs, HRD issues by the utilization of a HR. Specifically; we are keen on what approach choices will create for the arrangement of prevailing HR issues in SMEs.

Assessing the writing on HRD in SMEs we locate that one topic is prevailing: the genuine utilization of HR instruments by SMEs. Other significant subjects that have gotten substantially less consideration are the nature of SME-occupations (counting the assessment of the idea of mechanical relations in SMEs) and the conceivable connection of HR with methodology and upper hand and firm execution. With respect to utilization of HR instruments, a first perception is that researcher does not concur on the applicable components of HRD in SMEs. Research demonstrates that HR-rehearses differ exceptionally between little firms are frequently controlled by the philosophy and pluralistic objectives of the entrepreneur and because of its casualness, are increasingly complex at that point normally anticipated.

India's eleventh Five Year Plan has a reestablished spotlight on science and innovation through training framework which sustains imagination, R&D culture and esteem framework which underpins both fundamental and connected research and innovation advancement, approach structure which urges youngsters to go into logical vocations and growing new models of advanced education, especially for research in colleges and high innovation territories. The approach understands that peer looked into execution ought to be given acknowledgment through an appropriate plan of impetuses.

CHAPTER - 2

OBJECTIVE AND SCOPE OF STUDY

2.1.   HRD is fundamental apparatus

2.2   Human asset advancement and human asset technique in the SMEs

2.1   HRD is fundamental apparatus

The target of the examination was to demonstrate that there are critical for the SMEs to actualize the HRD. This HRD is fundamental apparatus to build up the SMEs in India. The hugeness of the examination is to increase the value of the collection of information on human asset improvement and practice. Explicitly for training, the discoveries of this examination would illuminate the essentialness HRD in the SMEs in India since the nation's gigantic advancement in economy has made it profoundly reliant on the assembling business.

From the hypothetical this investigation plans to broaden existing information of the HRD with explicit reference to the recently extended part in the assembling which is SMEs. The vast majority of the HRD thinks about were including colleges, global organizations, private firms, government offices, and bigger organizations. In this way, the present examination tended to the above contention with an end goal to build our comprehension of HRD in SMEs in India.

From the hypothetical this investigation means to broaden existing learning of the HRD with explicit reference to the recently extended part in the assembling which is SMEs. The majority of the HRD examines were including colleges, global organizations, private firms, government offices, and bigger organizations. Subsequently, the present examination tended to the above contention with an end goal to expand our comprehension of HRD in SMEs in India.

1. Identification of administrative fulfillment with the abilities of work compel
2. Highlight the HRD factors which are going about as deterrents in the development of SMEs
3. Evaluate elements in charge of the ability advancement of workforce
4. Identify preparing in different orders to make SMEs progressively beneficial

There is no acknowledged overall meaning of SMEs. In India, the definitions are exclusively founded on a settled quantitative measure; for example the complete number of laborers, the all-out number of capital, all out resources and recently by deciding deals turnover. The SMEs are additionally ordered into medium-sized organizations, little ventures, and smaller scale undertakings.

SMEs in India might be ordered into three parts;

(1) General business,

(2) Assembling and

(3) Horticultures.

The general business segment incorporates development, wholesaling and retailing, transport and capacity, business administrations and exercises, and giving administrations, for example, inn and eatery. The fundamental exercises in the assembling segment comprise of handling and creation of crude materials. In the interim the horticulture segment incorporates elastic, oil palm, paddy, coconuts, natural products, and vegetables. From the three segments; the assembling part developed as the most vital segment for SMEs in India.

2.2 Human asset advancement and human asset technique in the SMEs

With the assistance of this investigation researcher need to demonstrate the use of human asset advancement and human asset technique in the SMEs for their development and improvement. The examination isn't restricted with just HR system; it likewise finds the issues which stop the usage of HR procedure in the SMEs and their prospects.

This report is restricted in degree as there is an absence of learning concerning assortment of practices and ways to deal with HRD in SMEs, and as HR-specialists we need to endeavor to think about and comprehend SMEs. All together better to comprehend this size of associations, they must be drawn nearer as a heterogeneous example, where one will search for similitudes just as contrasts.

CHAPTER - 3

LITERATURE REVIEW

3.1 Commitments to improved authoritative execution with respect to other hierarchical ventures

3.2 The advancement and improvement of human asset

3.3 Advancement and improvement of staff the executives

3.4 Human Resource Management

3.5 Mankind's asset management: nature

3.6 Human Resource Management: Beliefs

3.7 Humankind's advantage the officials: emotions

3.8 Human Resource Management: Objectives

3.9 Human asset management: capacities

3.10 Human Resource Management: Futuristic Vision

3.11 Purposes behind disappointment about little organizations

3.12 Factors causative to business success

3.13 Human Resource Development

3.14 Method of reasoning of HRD

3.15 Critical Aspects of HRD

3.16 Hugeness of Human Resource Development

3.17 Triggers and inspirations of HRD in little associations

3.1 Commitment to improved authoritative execution with respect to other hierarchical ventures

Human asset the board (HRM), the administration of work and individuals towards wanted finishes, is a crucial movement in any association in which people are utilized. It isn't something whose presence should be intricately advocated: HRM is an unavoidable result of beginning and growing an association. While there are a horde of varieties in the belief systems, styles, and administrative assets drew in, HRM occurs in some structure or other. It is one thing to scrutinize the overall execution of specific models of HRM specifically settings or their commitment to improved authoritative execution with respect to other hierarchical ventures, for example, new creation innovations, promoting efforts, and property acquisitions. These are critical lines of investigation. It is very something else, in any case, to scrutinize the need of the HRM procedure itself, as though associations could by one way or another endure or develop without making a sensible endeavor at sorting out work and overseeing individuals. To wish HRM away is to wish away everything except the littlest of firms.

With such an essential dispatch, there should be ordinary surveys of the condition of formal information in the field of HRM. Altered from the vantage purpose of the center of the primary decade of the twenty-first century, this Handbook uncovers an administration discipline which is never again arriviste. Discussions that practiced us during the 1990s, worried about the coming of the HRM phrasing, with how it may be not the same as its ancestor, staff the executives, or with how it may undermine worker's guilds and modern relations, have offered approach to 'increasingly substantive issues: the effect of HRM on hierarchical execution and representatives' involvement of work. These prior discussions hold a notable job in our comprehension of the subject, yet the writing is never again engrossed with them.

Over the most recent ten years, the associations among HRM and the investigation of key administration have developed and interfaces with hierarchical hypothesis/conduct have developed. The writing on HRM outside the Anglo-American world has blasted over the levee, helping us always to remember the diverse socio-political settings in which HRM is installed. A procedure of developing has been occurring which we confirm in this Handbook. Looking outwards, the order is progressively mindful of various conditions, and is the better for it. Looking inwards, it is progressively worried about collaborations, with cause impact chains, with how the executive's activities enroll representative help, or neglect to do as such, and is the better for it. There are significant difficulties for hypothesis and philosophy yet we wish to concrete these directions: they imply that HRM is ready to expect a more noteworthy job in the hypothesis of hierarchical viability.

Human asset the board as a training happens wherever there is more than one individual. It begins at the family level where relatives take distinctive jobs and obligations regarding the achievement of family targets. The leader of the family would outfit every single accessible asset including individuals to locate the best in them so as to accomplish whatever might be required or wanted. In reality, the division of work relies upon the methods of insight, qualities and desires for relatives and which are established in the more extensive society, be it a group, a clan or religion.

3.2 The advancement and improvement of human asset

Overseeing individuals in a hierarchical setting is all around archived since the commencement of humanity. Authoritative structures advanced, administration developed or was shaped, jobs and obligations were allocated to individuals, responsibility frameworks were set down, and rewards and disciplines were additionally given. In such manner, division of work, specialization, and responsibility were deliberately sorted out to accomplish a particular reason.

Be that as it may, the documentation of the advancement and improvement of human asset the executives practices can be followed back to the blasting European economy of the 1900s. This economy made the fundamental condition for progressively genuine idea on the job of viable individuals the board in the developing work market of the time. The economies were getting ready for the First World War and its outcome where modern generation required a mass of talented, efficient, and trained work constrain. The difficulties rotated around assembly of assets including individuals, which prompted the advancement and improvement of four phases in overseeing work. The stages were for the most part recognized by taking a gander at the changing titles of officers in charge of dealing with the workforce and diverse jobs that were rising after some time. In this way, despite the fact that faculty the executives writing frequently states specific dates or many years of change starting with one stage then onto the next, as an issue of guideline, such dates or decades are more for accommodation and reference purposes than being real recorded occasions. A similar acknowledgment is utilized to give an image of the order of the advancement and improvement of human asset the board as we see it today.

Welfare organize in mechanical age verifiably, the 1900s was a period of expanding mechanical and monetary leap forward emerging from proceeded with headway as a rule and logical information through inventiveness and advancements. Undoubtedly, the headways had genuine effect on financial development and interest for merchandise and ventures in Europe and in Germany specifically for the arrangements of World War I. More merchandise was requested, and the huge generation of products should be possible more proficiently than any other time in recent memory, under one modern rooftop.

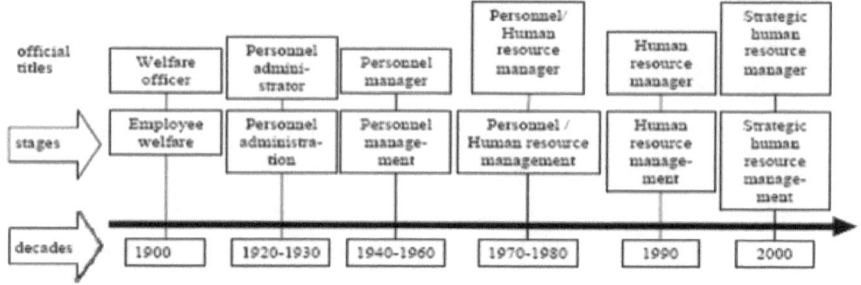

Figure: Stages in the advancement and
improvement of human asset the executives

3.3 Advancement and improvement of staff the executives

This covers the period amid and after World War II. During the 50s, there was a regularly developing job for work force organization to adapt to the rising difficulties and requests of the activity which included specialty, supervisory preparing and work debate that were compromising representatives and authoritative effectiveness. These new measurements in worker the board were exacerbated by advancements in the scholarly world, proficient directors keen on scholastics and specialists where endeavors were dedicated to consider conduct factors in occupation execution. Such advancements incorporate human relations' school that accentuated on enhancing the workplace and work bunches as a system to enhance efficiency. Regarding representatives as individuals as opposed to working devices was another convention that was uncovering different parts of individuals the board in different periods of faculty the executives. This period denoted a move of accentuation from dealing with an individual worker to overseeing gatherings/groups in the association. Different commitments were from crafted by Abraham Maslow on the human progressive system of requirements and the intensity of representative's inspiration on profitability. Later about the idea of representative's fulfillment and the noteworthy effect this idea has had on the hierarchical practices in enhancing the nature of work in associations. The association improvement school driven by Bennis and Schein gave similarly valuable contributions to faculty rehearse especially in regions of viable correspondence and the need to lessen strife in the work place. Consequently, to suit the style of the time, there had all the earmarks of being a contrast among 'organization' and 'the board'. Moreover, there is a contrast among 'chairman' and 'administrator', where the previous seems, by all accounts, to be managing more with routine exercises, the last manages increasingly key issues. There is anyway an on-going discussion in the scholarly community on the semantics and the real substance of staff occupations.

Amid the 60s faculty the executives as an expert order developed as portrayed by most staff the executive's speculations, practices, and procedures we know today. Notwithstanding the administrations gave in the before stages, different territories canvassed in the elements of work force the executives, especially during the 1960s, were hierarchical advancement, the board improvement, methodical preparing, and labor arranging. Better procedures and systems of representative determination, preparing, wages and compensation organization and execution evaluation were presented. The other territory was modern relations in which staff supervisors progressed toward becoming specialists in labor law and spoke to their associations in mechanical relations debate.

In this way:

1. Work force the board as a sort of the board in associations has advanced into a particular order.
2. Maybe a standout amongst the most broadly acknowledged depictions of the significance of work force the executives is the one given by Michael Armstrong in 1995.

This definition isn't altogether different from the ones found in changed releases and different course readings on human asset the board all through the 2000s. Armstrong characterizes work force the executives as 'the procedure and routine with regards to getting individuals in association, evaluating and remunerating for execution, and building up their maximum capacity for the accomplishment of hierarchical goals'.

The work force capacities are outlined and clarified underneath as pursues:

A. **Establishment of the authoritative structure**:
   This includes:-
   1. Building up the association structure such that will empower the acknowledgment of the planned mission, vision, objectives, destinations, techniques, and assignments.
   2. It resembles an African saying that 'you scratch your back where your hand can reach'. No single hierarchical structure can suit all associations in light of the fact that the appropriateness of an authoritative structure will rely upon where the association is, and what its future prospects are.
   3. In the event that the mission of the association includes quick development and extension, a tall bureaucratic structure may not be alluring on the grounds that such a structure moderates the basic leadership process, which thusly, smothers adaptability, imagination and advancement.
   4. A work force officer who is in a general sense in charge of viable keeping an eye on levels in the association has the command to end up some portion of the hierarchical structure configuration group.

B. **Human resourcing**: Resourcing is an idea that has developed with the utilization of the term 'human asset arranging' as we will see later.

It includes:

1. A procedure of empowering the association to have the correct individuals, doing the correct employments at the perfect time.
2. This is in accordance with the difficulties confronting directors in staffing associations.
3. It is tied in with getting ready for the number and nature of workers required under various employment classifications and to ensure that staffing procedure, for example, enrollment, determination, position, advancements, exchanges, and scaling down are powerful.

C. **Managing execution evaluation**: The work force division needs to start the framework, procedure, methods and devices of individual, groups and hierarchical execution estimation.

It needs to guarantee that:

1. Execution focuses for people, groups, segments and divisions are set and settled upon and measures to address execution holes are set up and are working. This isn't a simple undertaking since it requires an esteem judgment about representatives.
2. Without a doubt, there are no different regions of faculty the executives that make work force officers more awkward and disagreeable than the evaluation work.
3. This is on the grounds that whatever procedure or apparatus is utilized to evaluate staff and reward them as needs be, there is constantly implicit, or unequivocal disappointment from staff dependent on the sentiments that such choices were one-sided.
4. Advancement has been made towards enhancing staff examination frameworks, which will be secured later under execution the board.

D. **Personnel preparing and improvement**: Since the execution of the association relies upon the ability of the workforce, preparing and advancement are critical, for the present employment as well as for the future occupation and association.

   1. The leader of the faculty division needs to configuration instruments for surveying the requirement for preparing that will be utilized to recognize preparing and advancement holes and create compelling techniques and projects for preparing and creating staff.

   2. In most huge associations and all the more so in government services, there are divisions and officers in charge of guaranteeing that work force preparing and advancement capacities are completed adequately.

E. **Compensation/Rewards the board**: The words 'remuneration' and 'reward' are frequently utilized conversely in contemporary staff the board. In spite of the fact that on a basic level, the two ideas may mean a similar thing, they have diverse philosophical roots. While the previous depends on the understanding that work isn't really something to be thankful for and consequently the individuals who work lose something which ought to be redressed, the later considers work positive and something which must be remunerated relying upon the amount and nature of achievement. Consequently, workers need distinctive sorts of pay or rewards for the exertion they use at work and empower the association work. It is the obligation of the human asset office through the capable officers to assess distinctive sorts and dimensions of occupations so as to create fitting remunerations or rewards as far as pay and other motivating force bundles.

F. **Personnel relations:** Connections between a business and representative and among representatives in the work environment should be supported to dodge clashes and debate which will at last lead to ineffective conduct.

1. The work force division is all around set for this activity as it has staff prepared in individuals the executives especially in mechanical enactment, work laws, and peace making.

2. Some mechanical associations utilize attorneys as modern relations officers; however qualified faculty officers ought to almost certainly play out this job. In any case, different specialists, for example, legal advisors and expert advocates might be counseled where important.

G. **Change to human asset the executives**: From the late 1970s and mid 80s we saw numerous improvements and difficulties which aggravated the dependability of financial, political, mechanical and scholarly condition experienced during the 1960s. These difficulties have impacts affected individuals the board in associations maybe more than whenever in mankind's history.

H. **Shift in worldwide full scale approach system:** The late 1970s and mid 80s was a period of neo radicalism in which showcase powers were a driver of institutional systems of country states and associations. This was a period when we seen solid contentions against direct state association in the economy. It isn't clear what the 'chicken' was or 'eggs' among lawmakers and scholastics or who these individuals, regularly alluded to as 'specialists' of the World Bank and the International Monetary Fund are, and what their job in the design and birth of neo radicalism and underestimation of the job of government in financial improvement is. Notwithstanding, whatever the case might be, the two legislators and advisors were imperative in the principle of neo radicalism. One of the first promoters of neo radicalism was the previous traditionalist British Prime Minister Margaret Thatcher and her partner moderate leader of the United States of America Ronald Reagan whose theories were known by their names, that is, Thatcherism, and Reaganism individually. They fiercely censured before liberal governments for causing the financial emergency of the 70s through intemperate government control of economies and overprotection of workers.

The privatization of state claimed associations:-

1. Unwinding of enactment for the private part and the inclination revenue driven augmentation turned into the new plan and both the ideal and required system for overseeing associations and the workforce.
2. Accordingly, costs cognizance and the strain to legitimize the job of workers in creating and supporting associations in the market turned into a test. Inability to react to these difficulties through appropriate work force the executives systems was viewed as an elusive incline towards the breakdown of organizations that had long authentic underlying foundations of fruitful business.

I. **Business rivalry:** The 1980s and mid 90s saw a questionable, clamorous and frequently tempestuous business condition. Expanded challenge from Japan, and other universal organizations with less expensive yet superb products was a test to American and European associations.

In response to the new challenge and as a system for adapting to the emergency-

1. A significant number of associations experienced takeovers, mergers, and business terminations.
2. These were likewise joined by overwhelming misfortunes of work, dealing with low maintenance, the requirement for people to end up multi gifted, and the contracting out of some work.
3. Somewhat as a method for tending to these difficulties the job of the work force master needed to change from responsive to proactive and from routine to key way to deal with the administration of faculty works to almost certainly coordinate the flighty condition.

J. **Change in client needs and desires:** An adjustment in client taste, design, and nature of merchandise to mirror their price tag put more weight on the associations to get the best out of their creation frameworks, procedures, and workers.
This must be accomplished by:
1. Getting the best individuals from the work showcase, create, remunerate, and guarantee that they are focused on fantastic support of the association.
2. So as to accomplish these destinations, an empowering domain for representative imagination and development turned into a need.
3. This new interest affected enlistment and choice criteria, staff improvement and reward frameworks just as the jobs of work force expert's versus line directors in faculty the executives capacities.
4. The job of work force needed to transform from that of a practitioner of staff capacities to that of accomplice in offering help administrations to different divisions to perform faculty capacities.

K. **Technological change:** Rivalry was likewise increased by the associations that could receive and adjust adaptable specialization advances to address client issues and desires.
The suggestions were:
1. Those associations had less, yet better prepared individuals, adaptable to adapt to quick mechanical changes.
2. Consistent learning and adjustment dependent on groups turned into a characteristic zone of spotlight on individuals the board.
3. Data innovation decimated learning restraining infrastructure.
4. The intensity of information turned out to be the manner by which best to utilize it, as opposed to who possesses it.

L. **Change of logic of worker relations:** The intensity of workers was through administered worker's guilds where a large number of representatives under the modern creation framework held power. In this manner, the intensity of individual workers in the business relationship was vested in an aggregate solidarity. Mass redundancies, less defensive job of the state just as the declining job of worker's organizations made life more individualistic than group. The difference in worker relations from community to independence was a programmed outcome of the above changes. Business relations turned out to be progressively founded on courses of action and assertions between the representative and manager rather than the utilization of worker's guilds and work enactment.

M. **Developments in the scholarly community:** Expanding on the learning amassed in earlier decades and research that was being directed especially during the 1980s and mid-1990s, it created the impression that hierarchical procedure, and vital way to deal with overseeing representatives was the best alternative for reacting to difficulties confronting associations (Hendry 1995). The Human Resource Management School, progressed by scholastics from America and Europe, which led the idea of 'vital methodology' to overseeing individuals, turned into the focal point of discussions and improvement of human asset the board as a theory particular from faculty the executives. The Excellence School propounded by Peters and Waterman and their devotees on the job of solid authoritative societies and responsibility to perfection additionally has impacted the improvement of human asset the executives. A few territories of corporate administration including the size, structure, technique, culture, item, and hierarchical life cycle were presently incorporated into human asset the board.

The serious issue was the way faculty the executives capacities could have an effect on the useful dimension, as a component of supporting different divisions, just as being a piece of business methodology. Staff directors needed to end up accomplices in the business. As a feature of enhancing workers' usage, an increasingly thorough strategy for surveying the execution of representatives in connection to rewards was additionally created. The presentation of execution the board frameworks and reward frameworks dependent on execution meant that adjustments in work force the board rehearses.

3.4   Human Resource Management

HR might be characterized as the absolute information, abilities, inventive capacities, gifts and aptitudes of an association's workforce, just as the qualities, demeanors, methodologies and convictions of the people engaged with the undertakings of the association. It is the entirety or total of natural capacities, obtained information and abilities spoken to by the gifts and aptitudes of the people utilized in the association.

The administration of HR (HRM, HR) is the administration of representatives of an association. This incorporates work and mediation as per the law and the mandates of an organization

Regardless, these standard explanations are ending up less fundamental for the theoretical control. From time to time even delegate and mechanical relations are confusingly recorded as comparable words, in spite of the way that these ordinarily insinuate the association among the officials and masters and the lead of workers in associations.

Those humankind's benefits would multidimensional to way. Beginning with the national side of the perspective, humanity's benefits may make described Similarly as those information, abilities, inventive capacities, gifts What's more aptitudes obtained in the populace; in light of the fact that from those perspective of the single individual endeavor, they address the total of the basic capacities, secured realizing What's more capacities as exemplified in the gifts Also aptitudes from asserting its specialists.

Humanity's advantage organization need come to be recognized Likewise an unavoidable and just administration, which is stressed with those humankind's benefits for an affiliation. Its target will be the help for predominant humankind's relations in the affiliation Eventually Tom's examining that improvement, arrangement Furthermore appraisal for strategies, techniques and projects relating to humankind's advantages ought to streamline their responsibility towards the affirmation of legitimate targets.

Over different words, HRM might be concerned for getting better results with the planned exertion about people. It is a fundamental examination yet prominent and just administration, stressed with people at work and their associations inside the undertaking. HRM serves in accomplishing most extraordinary one of a kind advancement, appealing endeavoring affiliation the center of agents also managers, delegates What's more representatives, and amazing showing from asserting human resources Concerning outline stood out from physical resources. It might be that enlistment, determination, improvement, use, installment Also motivation for humanity's benefits toward those affiliations.

3.5   Mankind's asset management: nature.

Human Resource Management is a procedure of uniting individuals and associations with the goal that the objectives of each are met. The different highlights of HRM include:

a.   It is inescapable in nature as it is available in all endeavors.
b.   Its emphasis is on results as opposed to on guidelines.
c.   It attempts to enable representatives to build up their potential completely.

d. It urges representatives to give their best to the association.

e. It is about individuals at work, both as people and gatherings.

f. It endeavors to put individuals on allocated employments so as to deliver great outcomes.

g. It enables an association to meet its objectives later on by accommodating skillful and very much inspired workers.

h. It attempts to manufacture and keep up genial relations between individuals working at different dimensions in the association.

i. It is a multidisciplinary movement, using learning and information sources drawn from brain science, financial aspects, and so forth.

3.6   Human Resource Management: Beliefs

The Human Resource Management rationale relies upon the going with feelings:

a. Human resource is the most basic asset in the affiliation and can be created and extended to an unlimited degree.

b. A sound air with estimations of responsiveness, energy, trust, shared trait and joint exertion is central for making human resource.

c. HRM can be masterminded and checked in habits that are useful both to the general population and the affiliation.

d. Employees feel concentrated on their work and the affiliation, if the affiliation proliferates a supposition of belongingness.

e. Employees feel incredibly fiery if the affiliation suits satisfaction of their basic and progressively hoisted sum needs.

f. Employee obligation is extended with the opportunity to discover and use one's abilities and potential in one's work.

g. It is every central's commitment to ensure the progression and utilization of the capacities of subordinates.

3.7 Humankind's advantage the officials: emotions

The human asset association strategy for thinking relies upon the running with emotions:

a. Human stake will be those in every practical sense crucial asset in the Acquaintanceship What's more camwood be arranged and stretched out to a boundless measurement.

b. A wanton air with estimations for receptiveness, vitality, trust, shared trademark Also joint apply is basic for making human favored point of view.

c. HRM may a chance to be facilitated and checked to lead that need assistance solid both of the all-inclusive community and the Acquaintanceship.

d. Workers feel concentrated on their fill in and the association, expecting that the cooperation spreads a choice about belongingness.

e. Operators feel remarkably vivacious if the investment obliges satisfaction for their basic Furthermore that is only a trace of a more prominent test raised entirety necessities.

f. Worker responsibility will be reached out with the open entryway should Figure Also use one's capacities and credibility more than one of effort.

g. It is every principle's commitment on surety those advances what's more utilization of the limits of subordinates.

Human Resource Management (HRM) is seen by experts in the field as an inexorably innovative perspective on working environment the authorities than the customary framework. Its strategies compel the executives of an endeavor to express their objectives with expresses so they can be valued and gotten a handle on by the workforce and to give the focal points expected to those to enough achieve their assignments. Everything considered, HRM structures, when really rehearsed, are expressive of the objectives and working practices of the undertaking generally speaking. HRM is in like way observed by different individuals to have a key work in threat decay inside affiliations.

Measure up to words, for example, staff the boards are sometimes utilized in an irrefutably kept sense to depict rehearses that are basic in the picking of a workforce, equipping its kin with cash and benefits, and administrating their work-life needs. So on the off chance that we move to real definitions, Torrington and Hall (1987) depict work urge the authorities as being:

"A movement of activities which at first engage working people and their using relationship to agree about the goals and nature of their working relationship and, moreover, ensure that the assention is fulfilled"

HRM identifies with those choices and activities which concern the administration of workers at all dimensions in the business and which are identified with the execution of techniques coordinated towards making and continuing upper hand.

Human Resource Management (HRM) is the capacity inside an association that centers around enrollment of, the board of, and giving guidance for the general population who work in the association. Human Resource Management can likewise be performed by line chiefs.

Human Resource Management is the hierarchical capacity that bargains with issues identified with individuals, for example, remuneration, procuring, execution the board, association improvement, security, health, benefits, representative inspiration, correspondence, organization, and preparing.

Human Resource Management is additionally a vital and far reaching way to deal with overseeing individuals and the working environment culture and condition. Compelling HRM empowers workers to contribute successfully and beneficially to the general organization heading and the achievement of the association's objectives and targets.

Human Resource Management is moving far from conventional faculty, organization, and value-based jobs, which are progressively re-appropriated. HRM is currently expected to enhance the key use of representatives and that worker programs sway the business in quantifiable ways. The new job of HRM includes vital bearing and HRM measurements and estimations to show esteem.

Highlights of HR the board is:-

1. People arranged.
2. Comprehensive capacity.
3. Individual arranged.
4. Continuous capacity.
5. Staffs capacity.
6. Pervasive capacity.
7. Challenging capacity.
8. Development arranged.

Human asset the board is a procedure comprising of four capacities:-

1. Acquisition of HR.
2. Development of HR.
3. Motivation of HR.
4. Maintenance of HR.

In the ongoing years there has been relative understanding among HRM pro regarding what comprises the field of HRM. The modular created by the American culture for preparing and advancement (ASTD) recognizes nine human asset regions:-

1. Training and improvement.
2. Organization improvement.
3. Organization/work structure.
4. Human asset arranging.
5. Selection and staffing.

6. Personnel research and data framework.
7. Compensation/benefits.
8. Employee help.
9. Union/work relations.

Staff anger cannot play out his activity in a vacuum as various natural factor influence HRM. Nature outfitted the large scale setting and the association is the full scale unit. Of essential significance here are the outside impacts of financial conditions, work markets, laws and controls and trade guilds. Every one of these outside elements separately or in mix can impact the HRM capacity of any association. The adjustments in the outer condition of an endeavor profoundly affect the work force. These progressions incorporate mechanical obsolescence, culture and social changes, arrangements of the legislature and so forth.

The outer condition comprises of these components that affect an association's HR from outside the association. Give us a chance to inspect these variables:-

1. Technological advancement.
2. Economic elements.
3. Employee's associations.
4. Labor markets.
5. Changing interest of employers.
6. Legal components.

3.8   Human Resource Management: Objectives

a. To enable the association to achieve its objectives.
b. To guarantee viable use and most extreme advancement of HR.
c. To guarantee regard for individuals. To distinguish and fulfill the requirements of people.

d. To guarantee compromise of individual objectives with those of the association.

e. To accomplish and keep up high confidence among representatives.

f. To furnish the association with very much prepared and all around persuaded representatives.

g. To increment minus all potential limitations the worker's activity fulfillment and self-realization.

h. To create and keep up a nature of work life.

i. To be morally and socially receptive to the requirements of society.

j. To create by and large identity of every worker in its multidimensional angle.

k. To improve worker's abilities to play out the present occupation.

l. To outfit the representatives with exactness and clearness in transaction of business.

m. To teach the feeling of solidarity, cooperation and between groups coordinated effort.

Human Resource Management: Objectives

a. To enable the association to achieve its objectives.

b. To guarantee viable usage and most extreme advancement of HR.

c. To guarantee regard for people.

d. To distinguish and fulfill the necessities of people.

e. To guarantee compromise of individual objectives with those of the association.

f. To accomplish and keep up high confidence among workers.

g. To furnish the association with very much prepared and all around roused representatives.

h. To increment minus all potential limitations the representative's occupation fulfillment and self-completion.

i. To create and keep up a nature of work life.

j. To be morally and socially receptive to the necessities of society.

k. To create in general identity of every worker in its multidimensional angle.

l. To improve worker's abilities to play out the present occupation.

m. To outfit the representatives with exactness and clearness in transaction of business.

n. To teach the feeling of cooperation, cooperation and between groups coordinated effort.

3.9   Human asset management: capacities.

In place to accomplish the over objectives, human asset administration undertake those Emulating exercises:

1. Mankind's asset or labor arranging.
2. Recruitment, Choice Also placement about staff.
3. Preparing and improvement of representatives.
4. Examination about execution from claiming workers.
5. Taking restorative steps for example, such that exchange from particular case occupation should another.
6. Compensation for representatives.
7. Government disability Also welfare from claiming workers.
8. Setting general and particular oversaw economy approach to authoritative association.
9. Aggregate bargaining, contract arrangement and grievance taking care of.
10. Staffing the association.
11. Aiding in the self-development about workers in the least levels.
12. Creating also keeping up inspiration for specialists toward giving work to incentives.
13. Reviewing Furthermore auditing manpower administration in the association.

14. Possibility examination.
15. Part dissection for work occupants.
16. Work revolution.
17. Nature Circle, association advancement Also personal satisfaction for attempting life.

Mankind's asset management: real Influencing Components.

In the 21st century HRM will be impacted by following elements, which will fill in as different issues influencing its system:

a. Size of the workforce.
b. Rising workers' desires.
c. Drastic changes in the innovation just as Life-style changes.
d. Composition of workforce. New aptitudes required.
e. Environmental challenges.
f. Lean and mean associations.
g. Impact of new monetary approach.
h. Downsizing and rightsizing of the associations.
i. Culture winning in the association and so forth.

3.10   Human Resource Management: Futuristic Vision

Based on the different issues and difficulties the accompanying recommendations will be of much help to the theory of HRM with respect to its advanced vision:

1. There ought to be a legitimately characterized enlistment approach in the association that should give its emphasis on expert perspective and legitimacy based choice.
2. In each basic leadership process there ought to be given legitimate weightage to the viewpoint that workers are included wherever conceivable. It will at last lead to feeling of cooperation, collaboration and between group joint effort.

3. Opportunity and comprehensive framework should be provided for full expression of employees' talents and manifest potentialities.

4. Systems administration abilities of the associations ought to be produced inside and remotely just as evenly and vertically.

5. For execution examination of the worker's accentuation ought to be given to 360 degree criticism which depends on the survey by bosses, peers, subordinates just as self-audit.

6. 360 degree input will additionally prompt expanded spotlight on client administrations, making of profoundly included workforce, diminished chains of command, maintaining a strategic distance from segregation and inclinations and recognizing execution limit.

7. More accentuation ought to be given to Total Quality Management. TQM will cover all representatives at all dimensions; it will comply with client's needs and desires; it will guarantee successful use of assets and will lead towards ceaseless enhancement in all circles and exercises of the association.

8. There ought to be center around occupation revolution with the goal that vision and learning of the representatives are expanded just as possibilities of the workers are expanded for future employment prospects.

9. For appropriate use of labor in the association the idea of six sigma of enhancing profitability ought to be intermixed in the HRM system.

10. The limits of the representatives ought to be surveyed through potential examination for performing new jobs and obligations. It ought not to be bound to authoritative perspectives just but rather the natural changes of political, monetary and social contemplations ought to likewise be considered.

11. The profession of the representatives ought to be arranged so that individualizing procedure and mingling process meet up for combination procedure and vocation arranging ought to comprise the piece of human asset arranging.

Vital human asset the board delineates that the significant focal point of the field ought to be on adjusting HR to firm systems. Human Resource Planning was one of the first to specifically propose considering an association's business methodology when building up a human asset plan. A Strategic Perspective' added to the establishment. These endeavors would in general take a current system typology miners, experts, and protectors and depict the sorts of HRM rehearses that ought to be related with every methodology vital human asset the board models accentuate usage over technique plan. HR are viewed as methods, not part of creating or choosing key destinations. A move in key administration thinking would be required to change that discernment and open the entryway for further improvement of the SHRM writing the dispersion of the asset based view into the Strategic HRM writing impelled this paradigmatic move in the perspective on the connection among technique and HRM. Since the asset based view recommends that firm upper hand originates from the interior assets that it has, the RBV gave an authentic establishment whereupon HRM analysts could contend that individuals and the HR of a firm could in reality add to firm-level execution and impact procedure plan.

This brought about various endeavors to thoughtfully or hypothetically attach vital HRM to the asset based view. HR practices may be effectively imitated; the human capital pool of an association may establish a wellspring of maintainable upper hand. HR rehearses joined into a general HR framework can be important, extraordinary, and hard to emulate, along these lines comprising an asset meeting the conditions essential for continued upper hand. A refinement between human asset (advantage originating from a prevalent human capital pool) and hierarchical procedure (advantage coming from unrivaled procedures for overseeing human capital).

3.11 Purposes behind disappointment about little organizations.

It has been referenced in Chapter Two the extraordinary commitment which little firms make to the economy however there are various issues that influence their smooth running more than their bigger partners. The word 'disappointment' must be comprehended inside a specific setting. Disappointment isn't really utilized just in the negative sense, yet a business could intentionally choose to close its entryways because of the proprietor director choosing to enter another industry, or because of lawful changes, or a family's choice to close the business.

Disappointment would be less likely within the sight of dimensions of training and the executive's experience. The way that little firms flop because of their restricted arrangement of administrative aptitudes infers that organizations fall flat for various reasons at various phases of their improvement.

<u>Most normal purposes behind
disappointment the accompanying</u>:

a. One-man rule – owner director who directions relate as opposed to driving them;
b. A non-taking an intrigue board which recommends support for one man rule; (not continually critical to little firms);
c. An 'uneven best gathering', with respect to its aptitudes base;
d. A weak cash work;
e. Lack of the administrators significance;

Organizations experiencing the above reasons for disappointment will probably utilize poor monetary data, overtrade and react severely to change, and will set out on activities that would put the business at steady hazard.

The explanations behind disappointment are not constantly known but rather inquire about shows the principle reasons or causes to incorporate, initially, the absence of capital. This is by all accounts the essential explanation behind business disappointment and it is viewed as the best issue confronting entrepreneurs. From a business perspective without sufficient financing, the business will be not able keep up and get offices, pull in and hold fit staff, produce and market an item, or do any of alternate things important to run a fruitful activity.

Furthermore, lacking administration is another ordinarily referred to reason. This specific issue is wide yet incorporates shortcomings as far as business information, an absence of the executive's abilities, poor or deficient arranging, and inability. There is an over-dependence on the single proprietor administrator of most little firms and there is a hesitance to move far from this administrative propensity with respect to the proprietor supervisor. This converts into poor HR rehearses where no new qualified staff is procured or specialist and obligation designated to different workers. Most little firms are begun in light of the fact that one specific individual is great at some movement or exchange and not on the grounds that they have administrative aptitudes. Chiefs of little firms should in this manner be generalists as opposed to pro and are subsequently in charge of distributing constrained assets and can't bear to settle on poor choices. The main driver of either private venture disappointment or poor execution is constantly an absence of the executives regard for key issues.

(a) Burdensome government controls

Sometime in the past little firms were absolved from various government directions however things have changed to the degree that similar controls looked by bigger enterprise are presently relevant to little firms. The controls are all the time mind boggling and opposing which is the reason little firms discover it so hard to conform to.

(b) Market Structure

Scientists have frequently disregarded market structure as a purpose behind disappointment since it is such an undeniable factor to consider. The sections of the market in which private ventures contend fundamentally on value, rivalry is commonly furious. The market will see the passageway of new firms and this puts weight on the current firms to perform. Little firms don't have the advantage of economies of scale which in itself could go about as an intense obstruction to passage for potential new contestants. Research has discovered that there exists a solid connection between low boundaries to passage and quick congestion in market portions.

An absence of learning of the market is additionally a critical factor that adds to disappointment. Be that as it may, given adequate time, information can be obtained. In a few examples information (as capabilities) is an essential in a few enterprises. For instance, to fire up a law office you need a formal legitimate capability yet to fire up a home stylistic layout business you can secure the learning as you develop.

(c) Outside Assistance

Where a deficiency of mastery in a private venture exists, this could without much of a stretch be enhanced by utilizing specialists or experts on an impromptu premise and there exists exact proof to exhibit the advantages of such an intercession (Hall, 1995). All the time the proprietor administrator is the person who attempts to tackle issues without considering outside help: the issue is aggravated by the constrained assets at the transfer of the private venture to utilize such specialists.

(d) Motivation

The inspiration of proprietors for beginning or expecting control of their business may have some impact in deciding their prosperity."

Though this examination won't concentrate on this perspective, it must be referenced as a factor affecting the achievement or disappointment of a little firm.

(e) Marketing

Showcasing is the unrivaled utilitarian territory that interfaces the items or administrations of a business to its clients. It is crucially critical to guarantee that this capacity is legitimately performed. Firms are bound to endure the profoundly helpless start-up period the less vulnerability about the underlying dimension of interest they would confront. The methods by which business was verified is imperative for the little firm.

(f) Financial Management

This must be viewed as a standout amongst the most imperative parts of business. Little firms have constrained assets and can't stand to commit errors not at all like their bigger partners. The money related data accessible to the proprietor chief must be nitty gritty; must be isolated from their own records; regardless of whether their budgetary data was gotten from a cashbook, bank articulation, twofold section accounting, month to month or quarterly administration records, and whether their monetary framework was automated.

3.12 Factors causative to business success

Studies are conducted to ascertain the foremost common characteristics of roaring entrepreneurs the 10 most common:

1. Technical competency
2. Power
3. Chance orientation

4. Initiative and responsibility
5. Integrity and liableness
6. Tolerance of failure
7. Internal locus of management
8. Human relations skills
9. High action drive
10. Creativity

3.13   Human Resource Development

Human asset is named as endless characteristic asset. An organization will grow just if its HR are produced accordingly on make them commendable for his or her employments. Human asset advancement, partner indispensable a piece of human asset the board, is more extensive in its methodology and doesn't relate exclusively in giving formal capability. Its methodology is hence planned that people World Health Organization wish to build up their abilities as administrators are incredibly made. They supply connect among aptitude and ways, which can encourage to exhibit the capacity.

HRD is partner present and nonstop perform. It's required with giving of learning advancement shot in order to upgrade singular group and structure execution.

Human asset advancement (HRD) is sketched out as a gathering of deliberate and arranged exercises structured by an organization to supply its individuals with the chances to discover essential abilities to fulfill present and future occupation requests. Learning is at the center of all HRD endeavors. HRD exercises should start once relate laborer joins an organization and proceed all through his or her vocation, regardless of whether or not that specialist is partner govt or a representative on a mechanical framework. HRD projects should answer work changes and coordinate the tentative arrangements and strategies for the association to affirm the prudent and powerful utilization of re-sources.

HR Development (HRD) could be a system for the development of human capital among an organization through the occasion of each the association and in this manner the person to accomplish execution enhancement. Adam Smith expresses, "The limits of individuals confided in their entrance to training". The indistinguishable explanation applies to associations themselves; anyway it needs a far more extensive field to shroud every territory.

Table: Responsibilities for HRD practices
in small and medium sized firms

sno	Responsibilities for HRD practices in SME's	Owner-Manager	Training Manager Officer	Line manager	Employee	External provider	Nobody
1	Identifying the type of training that's important to your company's success	82	24	36	30	8	1
2	Identifying the right type of training for the improvement of individual employees' performance	62	23	46	30	9	4
3	Devising overall plans for implementing training in your company	72	28	16	6	7	7
4	Designing training activities (e.g. workshops, classes, etc.) to meet the needs of your employees	41	28	20	6	22	17
5	Designing and developing training materials (e.g. worksheets, manuals, etc.)	38	26	23	9	23	17
6	Co-coordinating training provision with external training providers (e.g. Training and Enterprise Councils, colleges, etc.)	53	32	12	5	9	13
7	Creating a climate in your company which is conducive to learning	75	28	33	15	2	10

8	Negotiating and agreeing individual training requirements with your employees	62	21	44	22	5	4
9	Carrying out training in groups by presentations and other activities	38	28	24	8	27	28
10	Carrying out training by demonstration and instruction	49	25	48	24	23	5
11	Carrying out individual training by coaching and mentoring	41	21	55	23	11	10
12	Supporting and guiding individual employees' training and development	60	31	49	10	4	7
13	Monitoring and reviewing individual employees' training progress	63	28	50	13	7	6
14	Assessing individual employees' training performance (e.g. by testing, etc.)	34	20	35	7	17	23
15	Designing systems to collect evidence of competence	30	22	18	4	11	30
16	Collecting evidence of competence	37	17	36	9	8	24
17	Identifying employees' prior training and educational achievements	58	29	33	8	2	4
18	Evaluating the training plan for your company	67	24	11	1	6	15
19	Improving the quality of training in your company	74	28	20	7	9	9
20	Evaluating training carried out in your company	62	25	19	9	11	17

Table: Responsibilities for HRD practices
in small and medium sized firms

Human Resource Development is the incorporated utilization of preparing, association, and profession advancement endeavors to enhance individual, gathering and authoritative viability. HRD builds up the key abilities that empower people in associations to perform present and future employments through arranged learning exercises. Gatherings inside associations use HRD to start and oversee change. Likewise, HRD guarantees a match among individual and authoritative needs.

Human Resource Development (HRD) is the structure for helping representatives builds up their own and authoritative aptitudes, learning, and capacities. Human Resource Development incorporates such open doors as representative preparing, worker vocation improvement, execution the board and advancement, training, coaching, progression arranging, key worker recognizable proof, educational cost help, and association improvement.

The focal point of all parts of Human Resource Development is on building up the most predominant workforce with the goal that the association and individual representatives can achieve their work objectives in support of clients. Associations have numerous open doors for HR or worker advancement, both inside and outside of the work environment.

Human Resource Development can be formal, for example, in classroom preparing, a school course, or an authoritative arranged change exertion. Or on the other hand, Human Resource Development can be casual as in worker training by a supervisor. Sound associations have confidence in Human Resource Development and consider every contingency.

The general point of the human advancement is to see that the association has the nature of individuals it needs to achieve its objective for enhanced execution and development.

3.14   Method of reasoning of HRD:-

A few scholars article to the term 'Assets' being connected to people all things considered against the respect of man, who is really the client of alternate assets. Different masterminds feel that a human' being turns into an asset when he gets certain information, abilities and mentalities helpful for an association/society.

Means of Terms:-

Learning: Range of data regarding some matter.

Aptitude: Expertness in carrying out some responsibility. It needs practice, notwithstanding information.

Disposition: Predominant method of reasoning and feeling influencing conduct.

Training: Systematic exchange of information regarding some matter and ability of utilizing it.

Preparing: Systematic exchange of pertinent information and abilities to carry out a responsibility appropriately. Preparing is work arranged and by and large manages current needs.

Improvement: To bring from dormant/potential state to a functioning state. In HRD process it implies securing of more extensive learning, abilities and frames of mind to accept higher accountability. Advancement is individual situated and manages anticipated future needs.

Need: is a hole between the ideal dimension and real dimension. It might be Educational Need; Training Need or Development Need.

Hugeness of Human Resource Development:-

HR is the advantages which don't discover a spot for referencing in a critical position sheet of an organization. Be that as it may, it is one of the past essential resources as HR are an asset of generation just as they are using different assets of creation like a material, machines, cash and so on. Any venture made on preparing and advancement of individuals is certain to demonstrate the outcomes in the years to come. The consequences of any HRD plan or plan show up in long haul. When we manage improvement of aptitude, information and frame of mind, the advancement and advancement is an extremely moderate procedure yet not an uncertain procedure. The advancement of individuals for adjustment and enhancement in ability, learning and frame of mind has the accompanying attributes and thus it is probably going to be a moderate procedure:

1. It relies on the nature of preparing. How the HRD exertion will be arranged and HRD plans actualized.

2. It relies on the meaning of destinations which might be classified "learning targets?". In the event that HRD plans have obvious learning objective, the HRD plan or Program is certain to yield better results.

3. In the event that orderly and legitimate assessment of plan is done than we would probably survey the viability of the arrangement. On the off chance that assessment isn't efficiently done, the data won't fill in as information for development in future projects.

The advancement of individuals is to be seen appropriately, offering weightage to the way of life of the association in which individuals are developing. The earth and social estimations of the association would have an extremely noteworthy bearing upon individuals' conviction whether the improvement is attractive and felt vital by the general population themselves.

3.15   Critical Aspects of HRD:-

All assets of generation are critical like machine, capital, cash, land and building and so on so as to guarantee the accomplishment of creation of a running production line. Over all matchless quality must be given to the component of human asset as given above. The accomplishment of an association can be viewed because of collaboration and diligent work at all the dimensions of working of an association.

Any colossal capital interest in creating foundation of a preparation organization and its running will, in the years to come, demonstrate its outcomes in accomplishing higher efficiency and productivity.

Requirement for HRD:-

Associations should be dynamic and development arranged to support in the focused condition. This is conceivable just through the fitness of the HR. To adapt to the quick evolving condition, associations need to audit their HRD approaches consistently. HRD is neither an idea nor a device; however is a methodology utilizing diverse work force frameworks, contingent on the necessities and needs of the association. The fundamental supposition is the faith in human potential and its advancement by giving an appropriate and amicable condition.

Worry for improvement of individuals; have turned out to be critical for two compelling business reasons. Initially, rivalry in the business has constrained consideration of associations on expense of activities, affectability to showcase requests. These parts of business can't be served without full and thoughtful inclusion of individuals at work. Also, thought emerges from the amazing advancements in science, building and innovation. The new generation innovation, computerization and utilization of electronic control frameworks have changed the proportion of gifted and untalented employments. New frameworks require new abilities and certain base instructive capabilities. They need constant up degree of abilities. In this manner, improvement of individuals, decentralizations of basic leadership, compliment and distinctive administration rehearses than those followed in the past have turned out to be fundamental for survival of business. HRD activities address the issue of these business objectives.

A definitive reason for HRD exercises is "to have any kind of effect" regarding genuine costs, quality, amount, exactness and opportuneness. HRD exercises, all things considered, don't decrease costs, enhance quality or amount, or advantage the undertaking in any capacity. It is the hands on uses of discovering that at last can lessen costs, enhance quality, etc. It has been appropriately seen that "every person is conceived as something new, something that never existed. Each is brought into the world with the ability to win throughout everyday life; everybody has his own novel possibilities, capacities and confinements."

HRD is a methodology established on the conviction that individuals are fit for growth given a situation that encourages singular development. Development is, in this manner, imperative for hierarchical development. HRD is to make an individual, an all-out individual as far as aptitude, development, skill, mindfulness, change in accordance with the earth, and certainty. HRD can be viewed as rationality instead of as a program. HRD is for both which averts development and which prompts development. "HRD is the way toward expanding information, aptitudes, abilities and constructive work disposition and estimation surprisingly working at all dimensions in a business undertaking".

HRD is a procedure by which individuals in different gatherings are gained new capability consistently in order to make them progressively confident and all the while building up a feeling of pride in them. HRD is a way to deal with the precise extension of individuals' work - related capacities, concentrated on the accomplishment of both hierarchical and individual objectives. "HRD implies a sorted out learning knowledge, inside a time span, with a goal of delivering the likelihood of execution change". In the authoritative setting, HRD is a procedure in which the workers of an association are persistently helped in an arranged way to:-

3.16 Hugeness of Human Resource Development:-

HR are the advantages which don't discover a spot for referencing in a critical position sheet of an organization. Be that as it may, it is one of the past essential resources as HR are an asset of generation just as they are using different assets of creation like a material, machines, cash and so on. Any venture made on preparing and advancement of individuals is certain to demonstrate the outcomes in the years to come. The consequences of any HRD plan or plan show up in long haul. When we manage improvement of aptitude, information and frame of mind, the advancement and advancement is an extremely moderate procedure yet not an uncertain procedure. The advancement of individuals for adjustment and enhancement in ability, learning and frame of mind has the accompanying attributes and thus it is probably going to be a moderate procedure:

1. It relies on the nature of preparing. How the HRD exertion will be arranged and HRD plans actualized.
2. It relies on the meaning of destinations which might be classified "learning targets?'. In the event that HRD plans have obvious learning objective, the HRD plan or Program is certain to yield better results.•.
3. In the event that orderly and legitimate assessment of plan is done than we would probably survey the viability of the arrangement. On the off chance that assessment isn't efficiently done, the data won't fill in as information for development in future projects.

The advancement of individuals is to be seen appropriately, offering weightage to the way of life of the association in which individuals are developing. The earth and social estimations of the association would have an extremely noteworthy bearing upon individuals' conviction whether the improvement is attractive and felt vital by the general population themselves.

Critical Aspects of HRD:-

All assets of generation are critical like machine, capital, cash, land and building and so on so as to guarantee the accomplishment of creation of a running production line. Over all matchless quality must be given to the component of human asset as given above. The accomplishment of an association can be viewed because of collaboration and diligent work at all the dimensions of working of an association.

Any colossal capital interest in creating foundation of a preparation organization and its running will, in the years to come, demonstrate its outcomes in accomplishing higher efficiency and productivity.

Requirement for HRD:-

Associations should be dynamic and development arranged to support in the focused condition. This is conceivable just through the fitness of the HR. To adapt to the quick evolving condition, associations need to audit their HRD approaches consistently. HRD is neither an idea nor a device; however is a methodology utilizing diverse work force frameworks, contingent on the necessities and needs of the association. The fundamental supposition is the faith in human potential and its advancement by giving an appropriate and amicable condition.

Worry for improvement of individuals; have turned out to be critical for two compelling business reasons. Initially, rivalry in the business has constrained consideration of associations on expense of activities, affectability to showcase requests. These parts of business can't be served without full and thoughtful inclusion of individuals at work. Also, thought emerges from the amazing advancements in science, building and innovation. The new generation innovation, computerization and utilization of electronic control frameworks have changed the proportion of gifted and untalented employments. New frameworks require new abilities and certain base instructive capabilities. They need constant up degree of abilities. In this manner, improvement of individuals, decentralizations of basic leadership, compliment and distinctive administration rehearses than those followed in the past have turned out to be fundamental for survival of business. HRD activities address the issue of these business objectives.

A definitive reason for HRD exercises is "to have any kind of effect" regarding genuine costs, quality, amount, exactness and opportuneness. HRD exercises, all things considered, don't decrease costs, enhance quality or amount, or advantage the undertaking in any capacity. It is the hands on uses of discovering that at last can lessen costs, enhance quality, etc. It has been appropriately seen that "every person is conceived as something new, something that never existed. Each is brought into the world with the ability to win throughout everyday life; everybody has his own novel possibilities, capacities and confinements."

HRD is a methodology established on the conviction that individuals are fit for growth given a situation that encourages singular development. Development is, in this manner, imperative for hierarchical development. HRD is to make an individual, an all out individual as far as aptitude, development, skill, mindfulness, change in accordance with the earth, and certainty. HRD can be viewed as rationality instead of as a program. HRD is for both which averts development and which prompts development. "HRD is the way toward expanding information, aptitudes, abilities and constructive work disposition and estimation surprisingly working at all dimensions in a business undertaking".

HRD is a procedure by which individuals in different gatherings are gained new capability consistently in order to make them progressively confident and all the while building up a feeling of pride in them. HRD is a way to deal with the precise extension of individuals' work - related capacities, concentrated on the accomplishment of both hierarchical and individual objectives. "HRD implies a sorted out learning knowledge, inside a time span, with a goal of delivering the likelihood of execution change". In the authoritative setting, HRD is a procedure in which the workers of an association are persistently helped in an arranged way to:-

a. Acquire or hone their capacities that are required to perform different capacities related with their present or anticipated future jobs;
b. Develop their general capacities as people, to find and endeavor their inward possibilities for their very own or hierarchical improvement purposes;
c. Develop association culture in which predominant subordinate connections, cooperation and, joint effort among sub-units is solid and adds to the expert prosperity, inspiration and pride of representatives.

Human asset improvement (HRD) as basically comprising of these three Cs: skills, responsibility, and culture. Every one of the three are expected to make an association work well. Without capabilities numerous assignments of the association may not be finished expense viably or with greatest productivity. Without duty, they may not be done at all or are done at such a moderate pace, that they lose pertinence. Without a fitting society, associations can't keep going long. Culture gives the supporting power and soul and soul for associations to live. It gives the oxygen expected to those 10 endure. Its utility goes to the power particularly when associations are in a bad position.

Numerous individuals are not clear with regards to the contrast among HRD and work force capacities. Therefore, work force directors are naturally being assigned as HRD chiefs performing faculty and modern relations work. Indian Oil Corp. (IOC), one of the main open part endeavors, has effectively executed its HRD program and has accomplished advantageous outcomes.

The essential guideline of HRD reasoning is the faith in –

(I) human potential and its advancement;
(ii) Optimum usage of HR; and
(iii) An agreeable harmony between business procedure and HRD system, i.e., vital arranging and HRD ought to go connected at the hip. HRD endeavors may will in general be inefficient exercise, if there are no chances to use the advancement of human ability. Thus, all vital alternatives as far as marketable strategies will stay unfulfilled, if HR is not made accessible to execute them.

Harrison makes a connection between casual preparing, implied aptitudes and the poaching of prepared work in little associations. In asserting that pivotal, inferred abilities are especially defenseless in little associations, she offers, maybe, a method of reasoning for little associations not to prepare and build up their workforce. She composes:

When an aptitude winds up unequivocal, and deliberately based preparing can be accommodated it, at that point the expertise ends up versatile and can be poached or replicated by different associations.

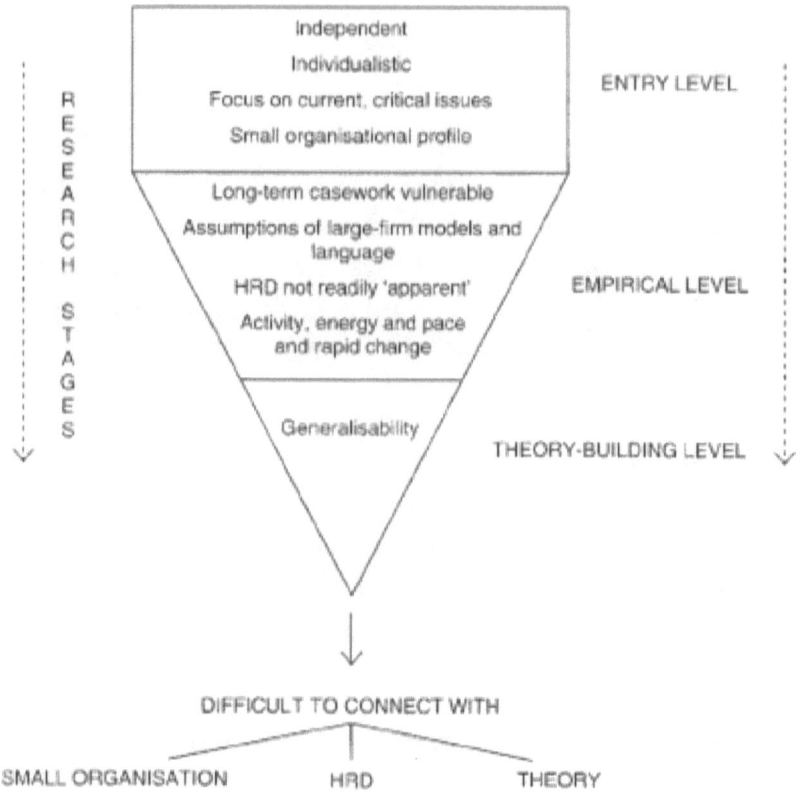

Figure: A theory of why HRD in SME's may
have become a neglected field of study

3.17 Triggers and inspirations of HRD in little associations:-

1. Strategy: preparing can mirror association's vision and system.
2. Growth: fast development or goals for development require staff enlistment or potentially procurement of new abilities.

3. Innovation: the association is a trend-setter and endeavors to work inside specialty markets.
4. Link to business execution: preparing can be appeared to harvest business upgrades and expenses of preparing are adjusted against main concern return on execution.
5. Owner-chef viewpoints: proprietor supervisor has a constructive ordeal of or standpoint towards T&D; or potentially knows about/has involvement of HRD issues; and additionally is accomplished/prepared/qualified by and by.
6. Culture: the hierarchical or the board culture is identified with preparing.
7. Recruitment troubles: where enlistment of talented work is obliged by economic situations.
8. Technology: there is new innovation in the firm.
9. Firm size: bigger associations cause lower unit costs in preparing staff.
10. Industry segment: formal working environment preparing more probable in assembling than administration division firms.
11. Nature of preparing: preparing is made applicable to the little association's assorted needs and conveyed nearby in adaptable structure.
12. Change activities: preparing is more probable when the firm is embraced change projects, for example, client care, ISO 9000, Investors in People, NVQs, execution related.
13. Expectations: there is a workforce desire and want for improvement.
14. External help: preparing is almost certain where 'great' outer help is accessible (for example fitting little firm consultancy)
15. Rationale for preparing: preparing is attempted to guarantee that the activity is done 'in our direction'.

Boundary of HRD in little associations:-

1. Inability to exhibit clear connection among T&D and execution in little associations.
2. Owner-chiefs dread poaching of prepared staff enrollment as well as staff and abilities.
3. Employees not keen on preparing as they don't need additionally preparing to carry out their responsibilities better or there is no advancement at any rate in the event that they do progress.
4. Training evaluated as unessential or immaterial to the business with no evident organization benefits. Business people have no genuine want for preparing.
5. Lack of inward HRD mindfulness/mastery to incorporate absence of preparing examination and arranging abilities. Cost of preparing both as far as genuine expense and time far from the activity.
6. Owner-administrators unmindful of the advantages of preparing.
7. Owner-chiefs themselves are not accomplished and additionally have no formal capabilities.
8. Owner-chiefs more worried about momentary survival issues than T&D issues.
9. Due to the different nature and restricted numbers on instructional classes, the expense of providing preparing to little firms is higher.
10. It is increasingly hard to supply preparing to an assortment of little associations that may be at different phases of improvement. Advancement is more outlandish in little associations than bigger ones – this is especially important to directors.

Where T&D can be appeared to procure business enhancements this is a potential trigger or spark, though a failure to show any connection is viewed as a hindrance. Little associations execute HRD as they see essential for survival, development and the achievement of business goals. HRD does not occur in little associations because of obliviousness of the advantages. Be that as it may, what are the advantages of HRD to a little association? Who sets the criteria for such advantages – the little associations or the individuals who give the T&D? All things considered, proprietor supervisors of little associations consider HRD to be an unfortunate obligation instead of as an end in itself, and view the accessibility of outer arrangement not even a convincing motivation to prepare yet more as help when and how proper. Little associations may casually and naturally break down their T&D needs at any rate, instinctually centering upon business points and enhanced execution. This strengthens prior perspectives that HRD exercises in little associations may not be viewed as 'legitimate preparing' yet as a feature of regular day to day existence, with 'the activity' accidentally conveyed as both a facilitator and a focal point of learning.

A substitute conceptualization of HRD in little associations:-

The previous demonstrates that customary conceptualizations of HRD may not be suitable for little associations, and a substitute conceptualization is created here. It is situated in a major recommendation that learning is (or ought to be) the focal point of HRD. In educating that learning is the concentration with respect to HRD and that learning happens normally among people, positions HRD as 'basically an intercession in the common learning procedure of associations and people'. In a little association specifically, where the proprietor administrator may trust that learning is natural inside the activity, it is conceivable that the activity itself may verifiably turn into a HRD mediation. The proprietor supervisor of a little association may, nonetheless, be more comfortable and OK with T&D than HRD and be increasingly disposed to dismiss formal preparing projects and worker improvement structures for casual preparing and normal learning forms. Utilization of the terms 'T&D' and 'HRD' mirror that position: that is, they are utilized to mean the equivalent. This perceives the likelihood that HRD is bound to be seen and discussed in a little association as T&D. It additionally perceives a potential trouble in attempting to mark and investigate a marvel (HRD in little associations) that clearly does not exist. It is further contended here that the classification of HRD might be of auxiliary significance to what HRD, as marked in a specific setting, may accomplish. In this sense, HRD is situated as a processor, or mediation in a little association's common taking in procedures emerging from normally happening hierarchical circumstances. This agrees with a prior proposal that, in a little association, the activity itself may serve to end up a HRD intercession.

Considering HRD a natural segment implanted inside a little association's foundation and ordinary schedules appears a more helpful conceptualization than its typical indication in increasingly customary systems and exercises, for example, off the activity preparing and formal chief improvement programs. Figure 2.1 recommends how the 'HRD' connection between 'little association framework and typical schedules' and a 'little association's characteristic learning procedures' may preclude the advancement of an ordinary idea and language of little association HRD, a view that could clarify why little associations show up not to 'do' HRD. Put another way, 'HRD' happening through the activity as a feature of typical work and critical thinking schedules isn't deliberately thought of as HRD, and accordingly is probably going to be spoken about by proprietor chiefs as far as 'the same old thing' and not HRD.

As likewise showed in Figure, new information produced will regularly be implied dominatingly instinctive, emotional and consequently sent in the ensuing establishment of hands on aptitudes and conduct.

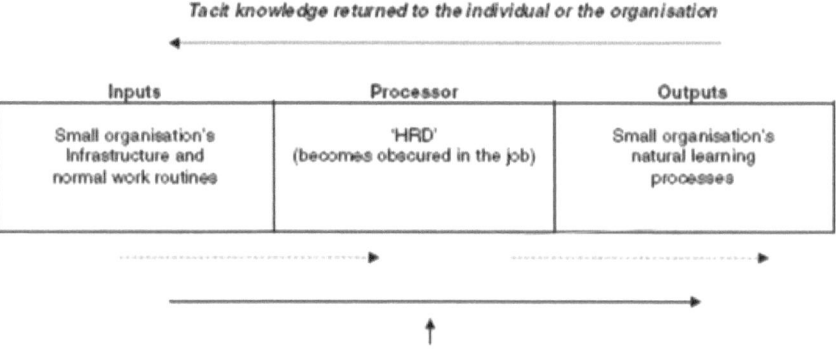

Figure: HRD in small organization

The reason and objective of research is to discover answers of request through its use of legitimate approach. The essential purpose of research is to find reality which has been found yet. In spite of the way that associated research consider has objectives fall into the going with general groupings:

1. To gain nature with a marvel to achieve new comprehension into it.
2. To delineate definitely the qualities of a particular individual, situation or in a social affair.

Research procedure, thusly, has various estimations; it has an increasingly broad degree. Research framework fuses the investigation methodologies just as considers the basis behind the systems concerning ask about examination and associates in elucidating a particular methodology or strategy is being used and why not others. To proceed with concentrate the right way it is essential to pick a reasonable procedure. Decision of technique is again a careful work and should be done with fitting understanding.

The word investigate is gotten from the Latin word significance to know. It is an organized and a replicable strategy which perceives and describes issues, inside decided breaking points. It uses particularly organized procedure to assemble the data and examinations the results. It spreads the disclosures to add to aggregate up able learning.

RESEARCH DESIGN & APPLIED METHODOLOGY

The reason and goal of research is to find answers of inquiries through its utilization of logical methodology. The primary point of research is to discover reality which has been found yet. Despite the fact that connected research consider has goals fall into the accompanying general groupings:

☐ To gain nature with a wonder to accomplish new understanding into it.
☐ to depict precisely the attributes of a specific individual, circumstance or in a gathering.

4.1   Research technique

Research technique, along these lines, has numerous measurements; it has a more extensive degree. Research system incorporates the exploration strategies as well as considers the rationale behind the techniques with regards to inquire about examination and aides in clarifying a specific strategy or procedure is being utilized and why not others. To continue with concentrate the correct way it is basic to choose a suitable strategy. Choice of strategy is again a mindful work and must be finished with appropriate comprehension.

The word explore is gotten from the Latin word importance to know. It is an orderly and a replicable procedure which recognizes and characterizes issues, inside determined limits. It utilizes very much structured strategy to gather the information and investigations the outcomes. It spreads the discoveries to add to sum up capable learning. Research is an ORGANIZED and SYSTEMATIC method for FINDING ANSWERS to QUESTIONS.

Precise on the grounds that there is an unmistakable arrangement of methods and steps which you will pursue. There are sure things in the exploration procedure which are constantly done so as to get the most precise outcomes.

Sorted out in there is a structure or strategy in approaching doing research. It is an arranged strategy, not an unconstrained one. It is engaged and constrained to a particular degree.

Discovering ANSWERS is the finish of all exploration, regardless of whether it is the response to a theory or even a basic inquiry, look into is fruitful when we discover answers. Once in a while the appropriate response is confounded or justifiable, yet it is as yet an answer.

QUESTIONS are vital to look into. In the event that there is no doubt, at that point the appropriate response is of no utilization. Research is centered around pertinent, valuable, and essential inquiries. Without an inquiry, look into has no center, drive, or reason.

Research might be characterized as a recorded composition work. Recorded exposition work implies composed examinations of the subject dependent on acquired materials with reasonable affirmation and counsel in the fundamental body of the paper. It is the quest for truth with the assistance of study, perception, correlation, and experimentation. So, the inquiry or information through target and orderly strategy for discovering answer for an issue is examine.

The examination philosophy embraced for the undertaking can be expressed as pursues:-

☐ an broad investigation of execution examination was done to comprehend the technique of working.
☐ a set of inquiry were made which is quite certain in nature.
☐ all the reactions were examined and dissected.

Information SOURCES

The fundamental information about the task is gathered from the corporate guide, association's very own web locales, and web and from the record accessible with the association.

The information was gathered from a lot of surveys, independent explicit in nature. Each structure is filled by the worker of various SMEs in Delhi/Ncr.

4.2   Research Instruments:-

☐ Interviews (unstructured or organized)
☐ Questionnaires (sent or face to face)
☐ Verbal self-reports by students
☐ Observations

The fundamental instrument of specialist examine for information accumulation is the polls. It comprises of a lot of inquiries displayed to respondents. Scientist has utilized polls on account of the different merits yet as some other strategy it additionally has its very own negative marks as well. These are as per the following-

Benefits of surveys

1. It is free from the inclination of the questioner; answers are in respondent's own words.
2. Respondents have satisfactory time to give well thoroughly considered answers.
3. Respondents, who are not actually agreeable, can likewise be come to advantageously.

Vast examples can make utilization of and along these lines the outcomes can be made increasingly trustworthy and solid.

Negative marks of polls:-

1. It can be utilized just when the respondents are instructed and participating.
2. The command over poll might be lost once it is sent.
3. It is hard to realize in the case of willing respondents are genuinely delegate.

There is additionally probability of vague answers and elucidation of oversight is troublesome.

Research Design:-

An exploration configuration is the plan of conditions for accumulation and investigation of information in a way that mean to join importance to the examination reason with economy in technique. Truth be told research configuration is the calculated structure in which inquire about is directed. It comprises the blue print for the accumulation, estimation, and examination of information. In that capacity the structures incorporate a blueprint of what the scientist will do from composing the speculation and its potential ramifications to conclusive examination of information.

The significant target of distinct research is to portray advertise attributes or elements of HRD in SME. A graphic plan requires a reasonable detail to what, when, where, why, and approach to direct research. An elucidating exploration can be additionally arranged into cross-sectional and longitudinal research. Cross-sectional structures include the gathering of data from an example of populace components and a solitary point in time. Interestingly, in longitudinal plans rehashed estimations are gone up against a settled example. Easygoing examination is intended for the basic role of acquiring proof about circumstances and logical results (easygoing) connections.

Research Design:

In research, analyst has mulled over the various answers got from the 100's of respondents. Each inquiry was planned so as to reply, straightforwardly or in a roundabout way to the exploration theory. The poll incorporates general, simple to-reply, shut inquiries, so as to make the errands less demanding for the respondent. A second part alludes to

HR exhibitions. The fundamental motivation behind the exploration is emphatically associated with the appropriate responses got from the poll.

Essential information, through organized survey, were gathered from an example of 100 respondents, arbitrarily chose from among the SMEs in Delhi/Ncr. The exploration received a study strategy to gather information on the SMEs general HR attributes (Personnel Policy, Manpower Planning, HR Information System, T&D Issue), association execution, HR execution (representatives dimension of inspiration, instruction, normal number of preparing days, normal compensation, offices for workers).

All associations that have partaken to the overview were in Delhi/NCR. As we expected, the review exhibited that most of the appropriate responses originated from the little undertakings. Empowering concordance and work comfort by giving equivalent material favorable circumstances to representatives (rewards, prizes, proficient and relaxation offices, and pleasant work atmosphere) is an administration practice in SMEs.

Testing:-

People have since a long time ago polished different types of arbitrary choice, for example, selecting name from a cap, or picking the short straw. Nowadays, we will in general use PCs as the component for creating irregular numbers as the reason for arbitrary choice. Likelihood examining is otherwise called arbitrary or chance inspecting. Under this inspecting structure, each thing of the universe has an equivalent shot alone that decides if one thing or the other is chosen. The outcome acquired from likelihood or irregular examining can be guaranteed as far as likelihood for example we can gauge the blunders of test, and this reality brings out prevalence of arbitrary examining plan over the intentional inspecting structure.

Likelihood inspecting is of following kinds:

- ☐ Simple Random Sampling
- ☐ Systematic Sampling
- ☐ Stratified Sampling
- ☐ Cluster Sampling
- ☐ Area Sampling
- ☐ Multistage Sampling
- ☐ Sequential Sampling

Non-likelihood inspecting is likewise referred to by various name, for example, intentional testing, purposive examining and judgment examining. In this kind of testing, things for test are chosen intentionally by the scientist; his decision concerning the thing stays incomparable. As it were, under this inspecting the coordinators of the request purposively pick the specific units of the universe for comprising an example on the premise that a little mass that they so select out of an immense one will be normal and agent of the entirety.

With non-likelihood tests, we might speak to the populace well, and it will regularly be hard for us to realize how well we've done as such. All in all, specialists favor probabilistic or arbitrary inspecting techniques over non-probabilistic ones, and view them as increasingly precise and thorough. In any case, in connected social research there might be conditions where it isn't attainable, down to earth or hypothetically reasonable to do irregular examining. Here, we consider a wide scope of non-probabilistic choices.

Non-Probability examining is of following sort:

- ☐ Convenience Sampling
- ☐ Quota examining
- ☐ Judgment Sampling
- ☐ Panal examining

Choosing an example

Analyst must characterize the objective of the staff's utilized in the different segments at different dimension to played out their obligation in the separate field has been chosen an example. The inspecting unit taken as implies that must be studied by and by. Examining unit might be topographical or constructional or person. Different sorts of tests are conceivable; it tends to be comprehensively arranged into likelihood and non-likelihood.

In this report, HR and Senior workers of various SMEs have been focused on.

Test size of study

In this report, test size of 20 to 25 Companies, for example, M/s MAT Braking India, FIEM, Supertech and so on was chosen for the review and examination was done in like manner.

Arranging and completing the hands on work:-

It includes a considerable piece of the examination spending plan and is a potential wellspring of mistake through absence of legitimacy and dependability. Hands on work techniques are managed to a great extent by the strategy for gathering information, the inspecting prerequisites, and the sorts of data that must be acquired.

In what capacity can Indian little and Medium Ventures Extension the Advanced Aptitude Difficulties?

India is one of the quickest developing economies on the planet and is relied upon to develop at 7.2 percent in 2018-19. As of late, business trust in Indian markets had expanded universally. As indicated by the quarterly 'Business Viewpoint Study' by the Confederation of Indian Industry (CII), the business certainty list took off to 59.7 in the fourth quarter of 2017, up from 58.3 in the past quarter. As the impacts of demonetization and the Merchandise and Administrations Expense (GST) that were taken off two years back start to die down, there indicate business standardization over all divisions.

The little and Medium Undertakings (SME) area which has been perceived as the foundation of Indian the economy is additionally expected to demonstrate recuperation.

Present Scene of SMEs in India

SMEs contribute 45 percent of India's Gross domestic product, as indicated by a report titled 'Small scale Dealer Market Measuring and Profiling Report', discharged by MasterCard and the Confederation of All India Merchants. This rate is just about multiple times what corporate India contributes, and it likewise demonstrates that the SME part gives work to around 46 crores individuals in India and is enrolling a yearly development of 11.5 percent.

Disregarding the gigantic potential it guarantees for the financial advancement of India, the country's little and medium organizations are tormented by different difficulties, for example-

1. Poor framework to expand creation limit
2. An absence of sufficient assets
3. Little advancement
4. Innovation learning holes
5. Absence of preparing and aptitudes
6. Powerlessness to draw in educated ability

The worries about foundation and accounts require cost-concentrated measures, and both the legislature and private area organizations are finding a way to address these. Different difficulties are firmly connected with digitization. These can be tended to through Innovation Information Exchange, a procedure through which innovation is spread from specialists to concerned people or associations to connect the computerized ability hole. Current approach activities, for example, Advanced India and Ability India, are centered on aiding SMEs turn out to be carefully proficient and train their labor to create vital computerized aptitudes.

SMEs need to cultivate advancement, take their organizations on the web, acknowledge e-installments, update existing innovative skill and contend all inclusive. Indeed, even with the quick reception of innovation in the nation, numerous SMEs don't have fundamental PC education abilities - making an advanced nearness through sites, mobiles or informal communities is practically outlandish for them.

SMEs work on low edges and reserves, and don't offer the most appealing compensations. Consequently, they battle when endeavoring to employ applicants with advanced. Thus, their supportability is under risk.

India is in desperate need of enlarging its development limit. While India has climbed the Worldwide Development File rankings two years in succession, regardless it remains at 66th position among 130 countries. India is likewise the third-biggest and the quickest developing online business advertises after China and the US. Be that as it may, to rival these two nations, it needs to improve its execution. The SME part is likewise ready to end up a $25.8 billion market for developing advances by 2020. Since SMEs can be instrumental in pushing advancement, web based business and innovation; it is basic that they grasp digitization. Thus, the endeavors to close the advanced aptitude hole should be fast.

Fortunately India has the biggest computerized ability pool on the planet, a reality that works very for SMEs. A joint review by Capgemini and LinkedIn uncovered that the advanced scene in the nation positions most noteworthy at 76 percent. SMEs will move to web based employing to take advantage of this ability to meet their computerized aptitude needs, and it shouldn't take long for ability to begin demonstrating measure up to inclination to joining SMEs as they do with new companies today.

Government Activities to Extension Advanced Ability Hole

The legislature has just attempted activities to help SMEs create and hone their computerized abilities:

The 'National Assembling Aggressiveness Program' urges SMEs to receive data and correspondence innovation devices and applications. It incorporates exercises, for example, creating web-based interfaces, giving nearby programming arrangements, giving e-proficiency preparing to representatives and setting up e-status focuses. This plan likewise sharpens SMEs to utilize vitality productive innovations and backings them on universal quality affirmation.

The '**Aptitude India**' program centers around teaching specialized, delicate, monetary, advanced and industry-significant abilities through hypothetical instruction, handy getting the hang of, preparing and extends. Be that as it may, this activity incorporates ventures everything being equal, with no particular push on SMEs.

The '**Help to Preparing Foundations**' drive gives a capital give to national dimension preparing organizations working under the Service of MSME to reinforce their framework and make business aptitude improvement programs. The fundamental motivation behind this exertion is to energize individuals, particularly rustic youth for independent work in SME area.

Industry Activities to Extension Advanced Expertise Hole

There is all the more uplifting news for SME ability hoping to secure advanced aptitudes. A few global associations have propelled real India-centered endeavors to give this area a lift.

Facebook has reported customized internet learning through '**Start-up Preparing Center points**' and 'Advanced Preparing' programs. The English and Hindi educational modules created in relationship with Computerized Vidya, DharmaLife, StartupIndia and EDII, is focused at preparing the greater part a million Indians by 2020 in different advanced promoting aptitudes.

In view of the discoveries of its joint research with KPMG, which uncovered that 68 percent of Indian SMEs are disconnected, Google has started a 'Computerized Opened' program. The preparation is ensured by FICCI and the Indian Institute of Business, and will empower SMEs to make a computerized character. The preparation is a lot of 90 self-guided video instructional exercises that are exceedingly pertinent to the Indian market. Google will direct 5,000 free workshops in 40 urban communities crosswise over India. Furthermore, it has additionally propelled a free portable application called 'Preliminary' that SMEs can use to increase computerized promoting skill on their Macintosh and Android telephones in English, Hindi and other vernacular dialects.

SAP India is additionally taking a shot at enabling SMEs to change to an advanced stage. It has marked a MoU with the Service of MSME to dispatch the 'Bharat ERP' program, meant to prepare more than 30,000 SMEs and young people on ERP arrangements. The organization has likewise set itself an objective of skilling, upskilling and reskilling 1.5 million SAP specialists in the following three years. Another of its projects, 'Leonardo,' will prepare SMEs and significantly bigger undertakings to enter the advanced biological community and convey development capacities easily.

Indeed, even HDFC Bank has acquainted advanced keeping money for SMEs with access credit, installments and different exchanges on the web. Its 'Computerized SME Bank' program will urge SMEs to utilize the web for all their keeping money needs. As SMEs begin depending on web saving money, they will get increasingly advanced abilities which,

thusly, will make interest for professions and courses in SME managing an account.

The State Bank of India (SBI) and Prophet have held hands for the 'D-Change' program. Volunteers from the two associations will advance IT education among school understudies and country youth to prepare the computerized workforce of things to come.

Improving Advance Abilities at SME Working environments

Before actualizing any advanced aptitude programs, SMEs need to direct an ability review to recognize expertise holes and assess the phase of digitization in their work environments. Does the organization need to begin from the earliest starting point? Are advanced aptitudes as of now effectively utilized yet require updates? This will give a thought regarding advanced preparation in the association. As needs be, SMEs can configuration suitable preparing and improvement just as enrollment designs.

Nonetheless, so as to do the computerized ability review, HR in SMEs would need to guarantee that it has top administration support. A best down correspondence would ingrain trust and validity among representatives in regards to the progressions relating to digitization. In the meantime, HR would sharpen representatives on how advanced aptitudes can be an individual resource for improve business effectiveness, upgrade client experience and procure better profession openings.

After the ability review and representative mindfulness creation, the HR group in SME work environments can take advantage of the projects started by the legislature and industry. It can likewise use online computerized courses and free instruments to build up their advanced aptitudes. Advanced Vidya, NIIT, UpGrad and SimpliLearn.com are a couple among numerous who offer complete virtual courses in computerized abilities at moderate expenses. There likewise are devices, for example, HootSuite, Google Investigation and BuzzSumo for SMEs who have fundamental computerized promoting learning and hoping to propel their abilities further.

'The American Express Worldwide SME Heartbeat 2017' study directed crosswise over 300 SMEs in 15 nations, expresses that 71 percent of the Indian SMEs are bullish about their local economy and 61 percent have idealism about the worldwide economy. They likewise comprehend the significance of innovation in driving income and gainfulness. Consequently, they intend to utilize imaginative plans of action and adaptable innovation in the following three years.

India's SME division appears to know where it stands and seems prepared to grasp innovation to overhaul its advanced abilities and enlist technically knowledgeable ability. It is currently up to the legislature and private associations to enable SMEs with an advanced workforce.

Hands on work of study:-

The hands on work have done by Mr. Almas Sabir and respondents really filled the surveys. Specialist had secured Delhi/NCR in this review. Specialist for the most part ventures Delhi, Faridabad, Noida, and Gurgoan for gathering the appropriate responses of his inquiries.

Cutoff:-

Telephonic meeting taken was insufficient to know the total data.

Because of riotous calendar, representatives now and again gave false data to stay away from it.

The workers did not react appropriately to the a few inquiries.

1. Absence of co-activity from the organization authorities.
2. Absence of time.
3. Absence of enthusiasm among target group of onlookers.

4.3   Information Collection:-

The precision of the information gathered is of incredible significance for reaching right and legitimate determinations from the point by point examinations.

There are two sorts of information viz., essential information, and optional information. The essential information are those, which are gathered a crisp and out of the blue and along these lines happen to be unique in character. There are a few strategies for gathering essential information, especially in study, distinct and trial looks into. Some critical one is Observation technique, Interview strategy, Questionnaire, Schedules, and so on.

Optional information implies information that is as of now accessible for example they allude to the information which have just been gathered and investigated by another person and which have just been gone through the measurable procedure. Auxiliary information may either be distributed information or unpublished information. It could be gathered from inside source or outer source. Inward source are which begins from the particular field or territory where explore is completed for example distribute broachers, official reports and so forth. Outer source are those starts outside field of concentrate like books, periodicals, diaries, papers and web.

4.4   Information Explanation:-

Essential information has been gathered through poll study which notice independently in indices. Keeping in perspective on essential information, the assembled information were progressively utilized. Along these lines our prime center is to accumulate the auxiliary information. Various sources are accessible and perused out in this point through Articles, Reports, Journals, Magazines, Newspaper, and Internet.

CHAPTER – 5

FINDINGS & DISCUSSION

5.1   Misconception Lifetime Learning

5.2   Favorable circumstances and hindrances for SME's against huge organizations

Under globalization, individuals will in general look for specialties in assets, and the outcome crosses national limits toward the most aggressive districts or nations. The substance of rivalry has changed from customary methods of efficiency to item quality, information, power, and advancement. Ventures in various nations demonstrate their solid motivating forces to create, select, and hold gifts. In the realm of free challenge, learning and advancement must be increased to keep up focal points in monetary initiative.

The test to Small and Medium Enterprises -Learning, power, and development as upper hands

Rivalry of the ventures in the new century will require quality, advancement, and speed. It isn't customary challenge in cost and amount. In the new economy, the concentration and guidelines for the activity of undertakings are drifting on wires of speed and learning. Globalized, internationalized, and enhanced corporate exercises are occupied with full apparatus. The existence cycle of items has abbreviated. The modern and capital structures experience fast change. Endeavors steadily lose their leverage in driving positions. Dynamic conditions request dynamic capacity for creating dynamic upper hands. "Knowledge" is the essential center asset. Of all other vital assets of an undertaking, the most profitable is scholarly capital. Just when an association consistently gathers, learns, and uses information would it be able to seek after determined advancement. This is the manner by which a venture can revive and open another time.

Worldwide mental ability is changing increasingly more quickly

The 21st century is a century underscoring progression and ecological security. It is additionally the era of intense challenge. New challenge and effects is from various corners of the world. The main unaltered law is change. In a focused situation where everybody is after speed, development, change, and survival tenets, people and ventures can't stay away from the test of the tide of history and time.

Scholarly Capital as Human Talent is exceedingly popular

"Learning" is as the standard for new challenge in the "post-entrepreneur society." In the new society, the predominant asset isn't capital, land or work, however information. In the post-industrialist society, the main social class is never again the entrepreneur or low class, yet the [knowledge worker] or the [service worker]. In the period of the information economy, learning is additionally [intellectual capital], which is the genuine center asset of focused power. In the event that one has learning, every other factor of generation will come into spot. Learning isn't just the prime resource of the association, yet in addition a basic factor that interfaces the upper hands of the association.

Interest in ability is principal to the aggressiveness of a country

In the period of the globalized information economy, human ability is essential to the intensity of the country; innovative work and advancement are the main thrusts for the improvement of the nation. Further, strategic channels are the connections to the world, and living situations are basic for individuals to redesign their nature of living. These are useful for the general public. Putting resources into HR advancement include: actualizing a broad English preparing program, completely executing on the web instruction, making a real existence time learning society, preparing and growing great quality individuals with global perspectives, great feeling of data innovation and development for the e-age.

The Outlook of Human Resource Development for Small and Medium Enterprises

Regardless of how the administration underpins the advancement of cutting edge endeavors or supports customary little and medium undertakings to change, predominant quality HR are basic. Hence, the consolation of little and medium undertakings to react to the patterns of advancement at a worldwide dimension, the foundation of the system forever long authoritative learning at a prior time, the motivation for creative thoughts, and the upgrade of center aggressive forces to look for the specialty for big business are the courses for guaranteeing supported monetary development in Taiwan. This is the inevitable mission and assignment of the administration. At present, this office seeks after the accompanying with respect to human asset advancement in little and medium ventures:

Arranges addresses and workshops for various types of experts in little and medium ventures

For helping little and medium ventures to upgrade their administration limit, mid-term courses were held for business administrators and expert chiefs: corporate administration, generation and R&D, human asset the executives, money related administration, and showcasing the board.

Sort out classes on unique points about new administration information

For helping little and medium ventures to get hold of new patterns, and prepared to assimilate new learning whenever so as to react to the adjustment in the monetary condition, this office composed workshops on various points of current patterns and money related administration. The prospects and measures to adapt to the progressions were examined.

Sort out preparing for the board specialists and oversee administration work force for little and medium undertakings

The reason for this undertaking is to prepare corporate administration experts with present day the board know-how and worldwide perspectives, just as set up the managing staff of this office for proceeding with training. This would assist the students with understanding the present circumstance of the business world and government assets better so they could give legitimate interview administrations to little and medium undertakings. This gathering of learners will turn into a solid reinforcement for the supervisory work of this office.

Little and medium undertakings are reluctant to put resources into the preparation of individuals since they don't have the limit. Moreover, it is troublesome for little and medium endeavors to keep individuals. In the wake of preparing various individuals legitimately, they bounce on board different organizations, or set up their own organizations. The entrepreneurs understand that they can contract great individuals with high pay, and in this way need not try doing the preparation and instruction independent from anyone else. At the point when this turns into a predominant esteem, no little and medium undertakings try to direct their very own preparation. They simply underestimate different undertakings. Huge ventures have rich assets and more open doors for advancement. In this way, they are eager to contribute as long as possible. With respect to little and medium ventures, they are not willing to do whatever another person will underestimate, and seldom pay for the preparation of their own workers. Numerous little and medium firms additionally don't enable their representatives to go to addresses amid business hours, which is a sort of abuse of the insight of the workers. Abuse or use and no further venture make the general population and information limit in little and medium endeavors blur away as time passes by. For the more youthful age, they effectively distinguish absence of chance for development and learning. This remaining parts a basic issue for little and medium endeavors in drawing in great quality youngsters. The negative winding impact makes little and medium ventures need ability.

Absence of the ideal individuals for updating and mechanical change

The generous enhancement of data advancements in the previous couple of years achieved success for the learning economy. Learning has turned into a key arrangement issue for some propelled nations. In reality, it is the pattern for what's to come. At the end of the day, data innovation not just rouses web based learning and replaces the customary method of learning information, yet additionally profits the Internet for online exchanges. This progressions the first method of business task and the pattern is foreseen. Later on, the development popular for a workforce in information creation and application enterprises will far surpass that in assembling of preparing Industries. To say it just, the interest for the workforce in the cutting edge space and creative works will increment, and the interest for the workforce in incompetent work and difficult work will diminish.

All things considered, we can see that the fruitful improvement of the information economy will rely upon the nature of HR. In this way, notwithstanding formal instruction, the arrangement of related supervision in helping the preparation of individuals for little and medium ventures through various preparing channels will be vital for what's to come.

5.1   Misconception Lifetime Learning

Learning is propelling constantly; this realizes huge advancements to innovations. The upper hand of today will be substituted tomorrow. Basically, little and medium undertakings in the nation are confronting quick change. For supported business activity, the most basic thing is to adapt new learning and upgrade capacity in advancement tenaciously. Be that as it may, numerous little and medium endeavors in the nation are occupied with the assembling of imitated items. Further, the vast majority of the specialists don't get a decent training. In this manner, just when the preparation framework is in real life and just when the proprietors of those endeavors get the preparations in any case can the representatives of those undertakings get the opportunities forever long learning.

Encouraging gifts can update the learning of people. It is additionally intently connected with the improvement of the ventures. For quite a while, the legislature has given particular treatment of expense conclusion, gave sufficient assets or different motivating forces to urge household endeavors to direct their very own human asset advancement. However, applicable writing and reviews on the issue demonstrated that with the exception of some medium and huge undertakings.

5.2   Favorable Circumstances and Hindrances for SME's Against Huge Organizations:-

They're here. They are immense, colossal. They have sharp teeth and need to eat the entire cake. They are the BIG COMPANIES. What are you going to do against them, you who have a SME?

On the off chance that that is the situation, and you have a little/ medium-sized organization or work in one of them, you are likely the most capacitated to reveal to us the numerous issues and a few points of interest that being a SME assumes on an everyday premise. What's more, you will realize that, in spite of the fact that things are never simple, being a SME likewise enables you to conceal a few pros from everyone.

In the event that, then again, you want to begin your very own experience in the business world, maybe it can assist you with knowing a few favorable circumstances and inconveniences of SMEs.

1. Focal points of being a sme
2. They're nearer to their clients.

It is a standout amongst the clearest focal points. Medium and particularly private ventures will bargain all the more specifically with their clients, which will empower them to address their issues all the more precisely and to offer a progressively individualized administration, and even build up some bond with their clients. When you know the business, the customer's connection with the SME will regularly is easier than with a vast organization.

6 Advantages and 7 burdens of being a SME's-

1. **They're increasingly adaptable.**
    On account of their size and less difficult structure, they will have a more prominent ability to adjust to changes. Furthermore, it will assist them with being nearer to their clients, which will enable them to know the varieties in the market before any other person. For instance, they will have more noteworthy capacity to lessen their supply in times when there is no standard interest.

2. **They can all the more likely distinguish and exploit little market specialties.**
    For whatever length of time that your eyes are wide open, a SME will have a more noteworthy capacity to recognize and fulfill unmistakable requirements of its clients than a substantial organization might possibly identify, or won't have an enthusiasm for covering, by being a bit unreasonably little for it.

3. **They can settle on choices quicker**
    In SMEs, basic leadership will ordinarily fall on an individual or a little gathering. This will make them significantly lither by making goals than vast organizations, where choices frequently require complex basic leadership instruments including many individuals and groups.

4. **It is less demanding to connect the staff to the organization**
    More noteworthy closeness to the board and a progressively worldwide vision of the business (in extensive organizations every representative's work is not so much exhaustive but rather more specific) will make it simpler to candidly interface the laborer with the organization's destinations. This will regularly build your inspiration, and along these lines your profitability.

5. **Everybody knows one another**
    Inside a little or medium-sized organization it is simpler to shape bonds and know the characteristics of others. This can be utilized to expand execution and improve collaboration. Likewise, in specific circumstances, for example, critical thinking, it will be a lot less demanding to share the errands among the general population who are progressively learned or better fit the bill to unravel them.

6. **Correspondence will be less demanding**
    By being nearer, it will be less demanding for the diverse individuals from the organization to speak with one another. This will empower new plans to stream and issues to be comprehended as a group.

INCONVENIENCES OF BEING A SME

1. **They have more challenges to discover financing**
    Ordinarily, SMEs don't have the money related influence that huge organizations have. Thus, they will as a rule need outer financing, which will likewise be progressively restricted and in more regrettable conditions, without the capacity to get to budgetary instruments accessible to vast enterprises, for example, posting on securities exchanges, capital increments, and so on.

2. **It might be hard to achieve an extensive number of clients and acquire their trust.**

   The assignment of achieving its clients can be extremely hard for a SME. The money related influence of extensive organizations enables them to make themselves known through broad communications by promoting, yet for little and medium organizations, achieving a noteworthy number of clients can be an errand that requires long stretches of exertion. Furthermore, being less outstanding than its bigger rivals, SMEs may think that it's progressively hard to pass on to their clients the security that a substantial organization can offer them.

3. **The expenses are higher**

   SMEs will have tremendous hindrances to profit by the economy of scale, which will make costs be higher in particular, kinds of business, just as making challenges to change the costs offered to clients.

4. **It is difficult to persevere through drawn out times of emergency**

   Regardless of being progressively adaptable in managing changes, the absence of money related ability can cause serious issues for a SME in the event that it is compelled to bear extensive stretches of emergency. Hence, amid financial miseries, little and medium-sized endeavors regularly face colossal troubles to endure, which causes the end of a considerable lot of them.

5. **Low dealing force with providers and clients.**

   Being a vast organization, and along these lines producing gigantic measures of business, gives a place of intensity while consulting with providers and clients. For a SME, it is significantly harder to accomplish advantageous conditions and is regularly compelled to give in more than they might want.

6. **Access to less talented work force.**

   Given the more noteworthy impediments that a SME for the most part offers to build up a profession (there will be less conceivable outcomes of progression), it will be progressively hard to pull in gifted and all around arranged specialists who will generally be more enticed to build up their abilities in a vast undertaking. In any case, this does not imply that a SME cannot pull in ability, yet will frequently bring to the table different motivators.

7. **They will have more trouble in getting to innovation**

   Sadly, and again for budgetary reasons, a SME will have more troubles to adjust to mechanical changes, which could prompt out of date quality. Nonetheless, there are fascinating mechanical arrangements that SMEs can get to.

CHAPTER - 6

DATA ANALYSIS & INTERPRETATION

6.1   Data Analysis & Interpretation

6.1   Data Analysis & Interpretation:-

Which factor affects the HRD in SME?

A1. Social & Organizational culture?

Response:-

Yes	No	Can't Say
84%	10%	6%

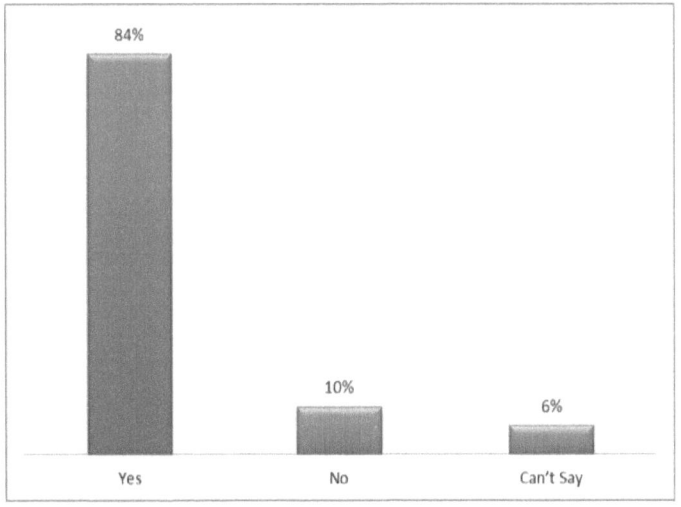

Analysis:-

In the response of question no.A1, almost 84% people say yes and 10% say no. It means that social and organizational culture is effect the HRD in SME.

A2. Personnel Policy?

Response:-

Yes	No	Can't Say
46%	40%	14%

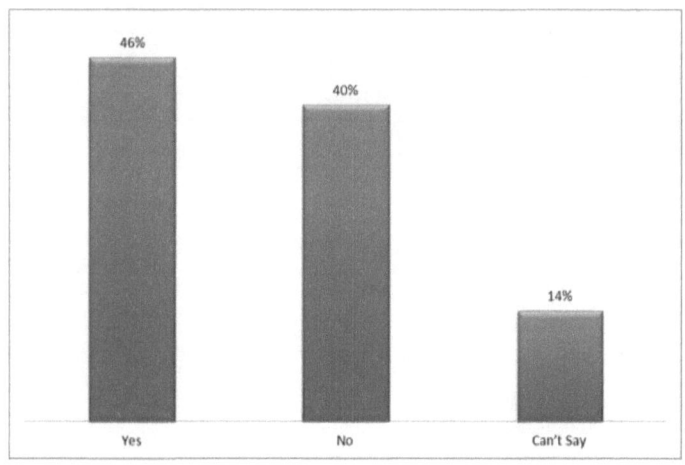

Analysis:-

In the response of question no.A2, almost 46% people say yes and 40% say no. It means that there is 46-40% thinking of people and personnel policy is not effect the HRD in SME. Some personnel policy which mainly discussed by the employee's are related to transfer, promotions, retirement.

A3. Recruitment and selection policy?

Response:-

Yes	No	Can't Say
10%	88%	2%

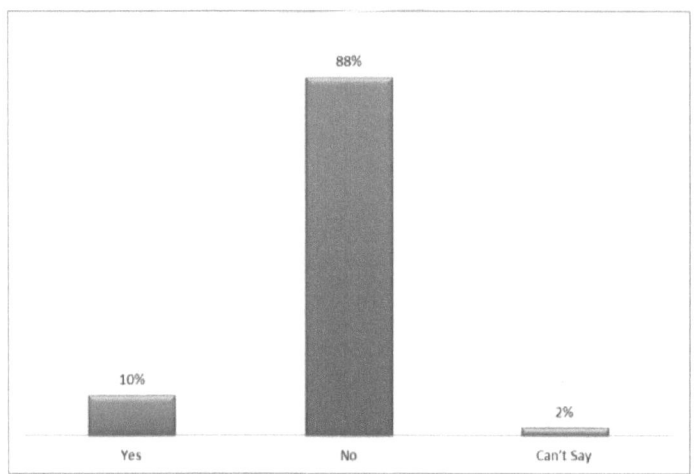

Analysis:-

In the response of question no.A3, only 10% people say yes and 88% say no. It means that there is maximum people think recruitment and selection policy is not is effect the HRD in SME.

A4. Training structure?

Response:-

Yes	No	Can't Say
86%	8%	6%

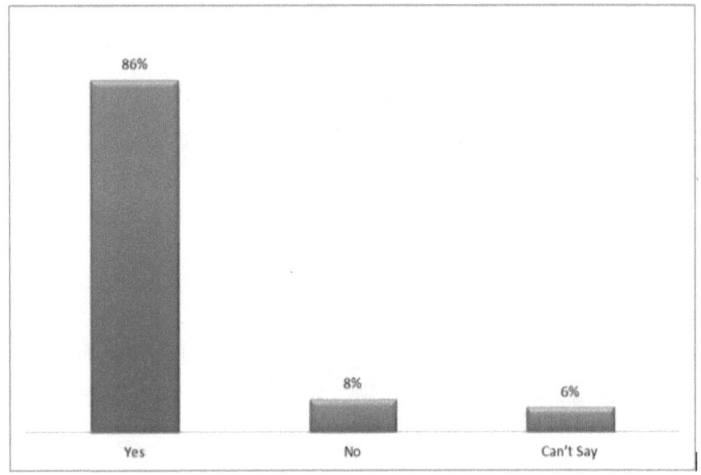

Analysis:-

In the response of question no.A4, almost 86% people say yes and 8% say no. It means that training structure is effect the HRD in SME. In these industries either very less training is provides or there is no training.

A5. Performance appraisal policy?

Response:-

Yes	No	Can't Say
48%	46%	6%

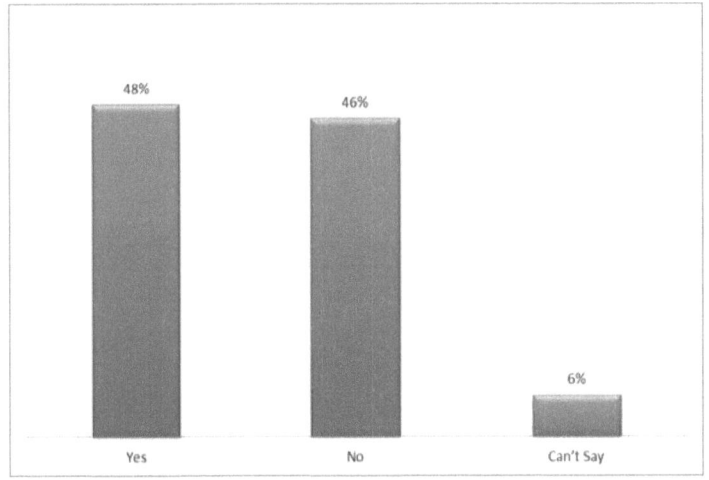

Analysis:-

In the response of question no.A5, almost 48% people say yes and 46% say no. It means that there is 48-46% thinking of people and performance appraisal policy is not is effect the HRD in SME but need some attention.

A6. Grievances?

Response:-

Yes	No	Can't Say
44%	48%	8%

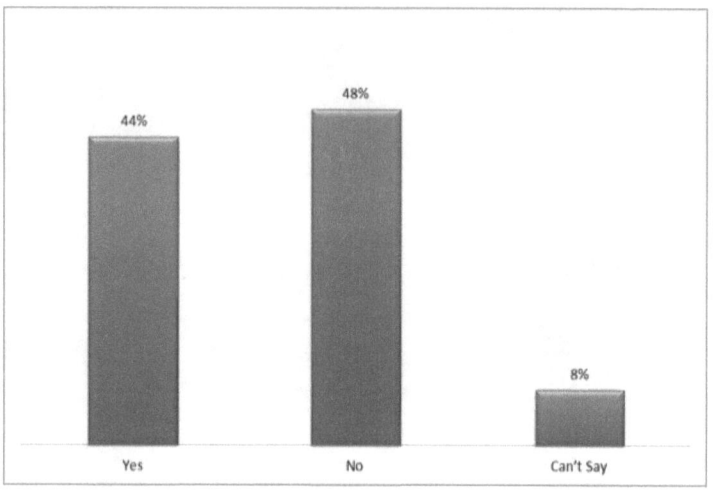

Analysis:-

In the response of question no.A6, almost 44% people say yes and 48% say no. It means that there is 44-48% thinking of people that grievance is not is effect the HRD in SME.

A7. HR information system?

Response:-

Yes	No	Can't Say
60%	32%	8%

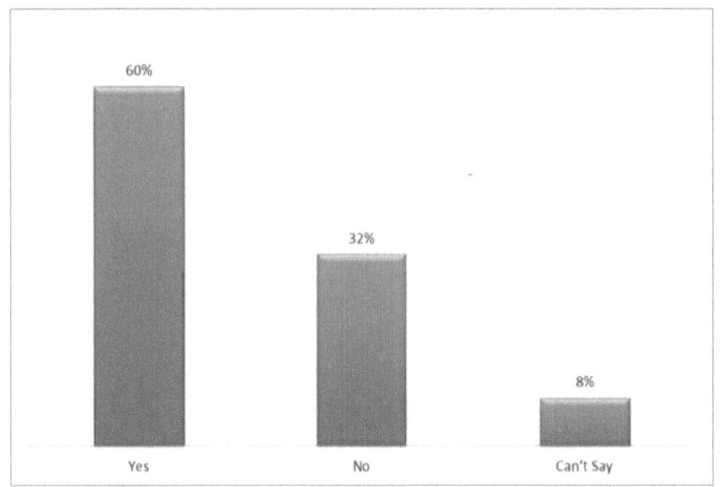

Analysis:-

In the response of question no.A7, almost 60% employees say yes and 32% say no. It means that there is 60-32 thinking and HR information system is also is effect the HRD in SME.

A8. Stress management policy of employee?

Response:-

Yes	No	Can't Say
82%	12%	6%

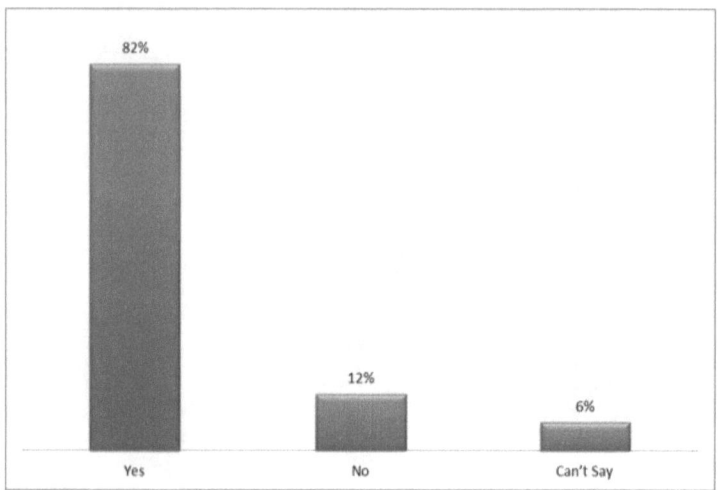

Analysis:-

In the response of question no.A8, almost 82% employees say yes and 12% say no. It means that stress management policy of employee is effect the HRD in SME. Most of the employees think that there is nothing which remove there stress (physiological as well as emotional stress).

A9. Mentoring?

Response:-

Yes	No	Can't Say
86%	8%	6%

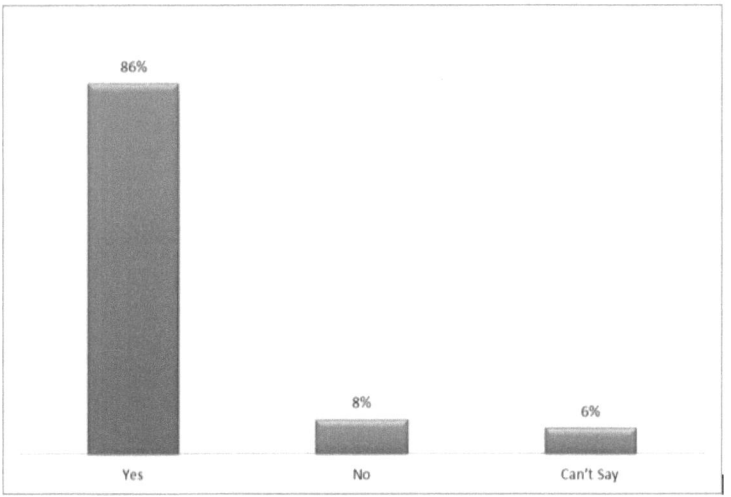

Analysis:-

In the response of question no.A9, almost 86% people say yes and 8% say no. It means that mentoring is effect the HRD in SME.

A10. Official politics?

Response:-

Yes	No
92%	8%

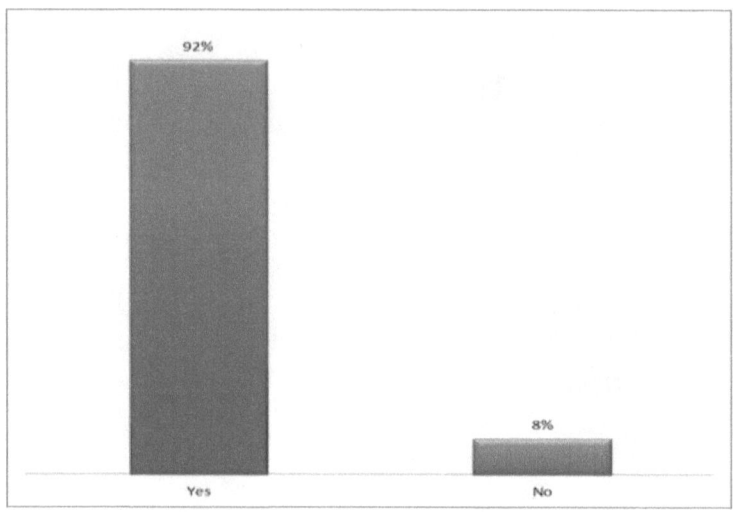

Analysis:-

In the response of question no.A10, almost 92% employees say yes and 8% say no. It means that official politics is effect the HRD in SME.

A11. Employees training

Response:-

Yes	No	Can't Say
82%	10%	8%

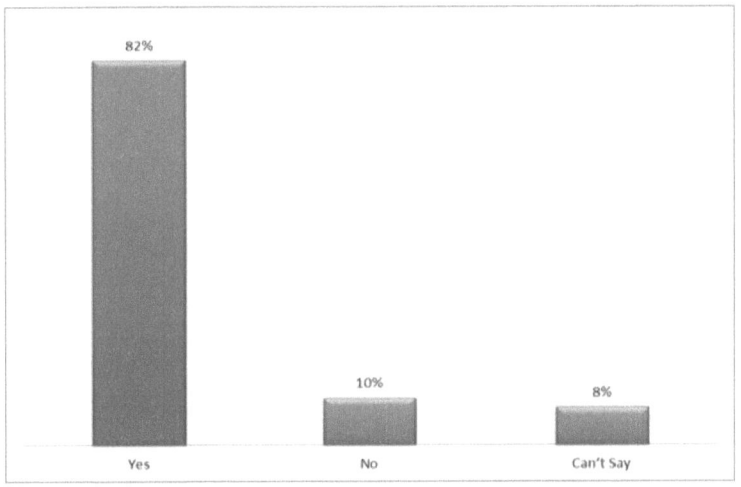

Analysis:-

In the response of question no.A11, only 82% employees say yes and 10 say no. It means that there are maximum people think employees training is effect the HRD in SME.

A12. Lack of internal HRD awareness?

Response:-

Yes	No
94%	6%

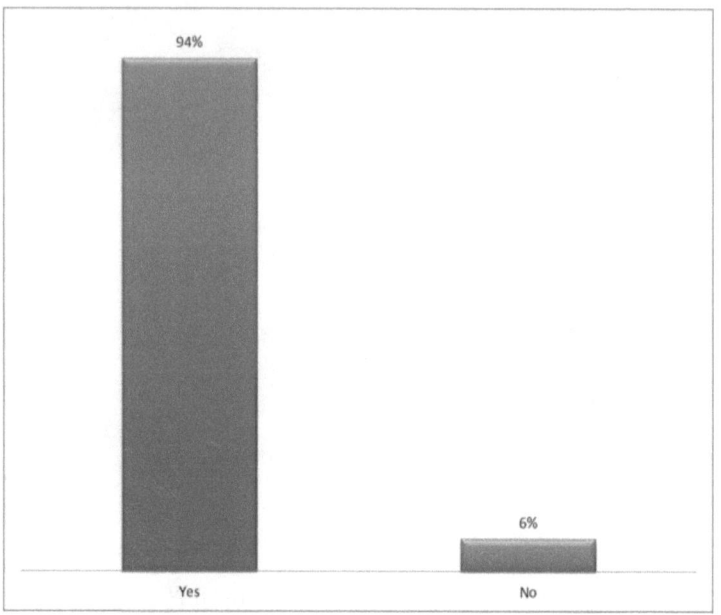

Analysis:-

In the response of question no.A12, 94% employees say yes and only 6% say no. It means that there are maximum people thinking lack of internal HRD awareness is effect the HRD in SME.

A13. Less educated owner/management?

Response:-

Yes	No
92%	8%

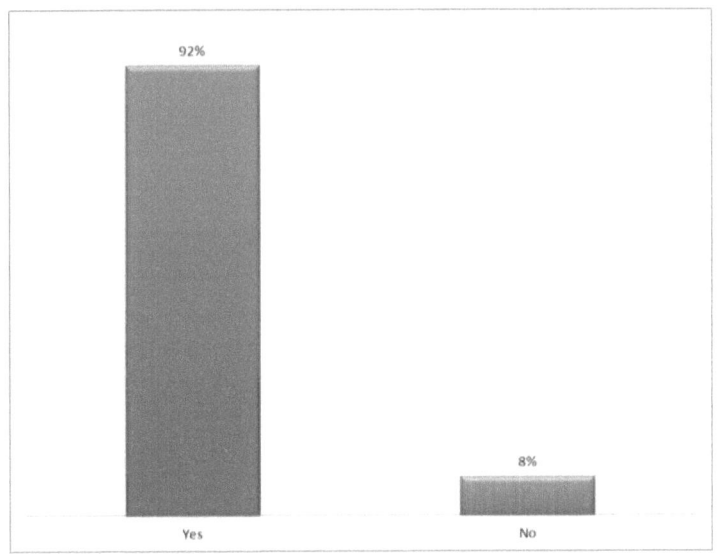

Analysis:-

In the response of question no.A13, 92% employees say yes and only 8% say no. It means that there are maximum people thinking less educated owner/management is effect the HRD in SME.

A14. More survival on short term issues then T&D issues?

Response:-

Yes	No	Can't Say
70%	20%	10%

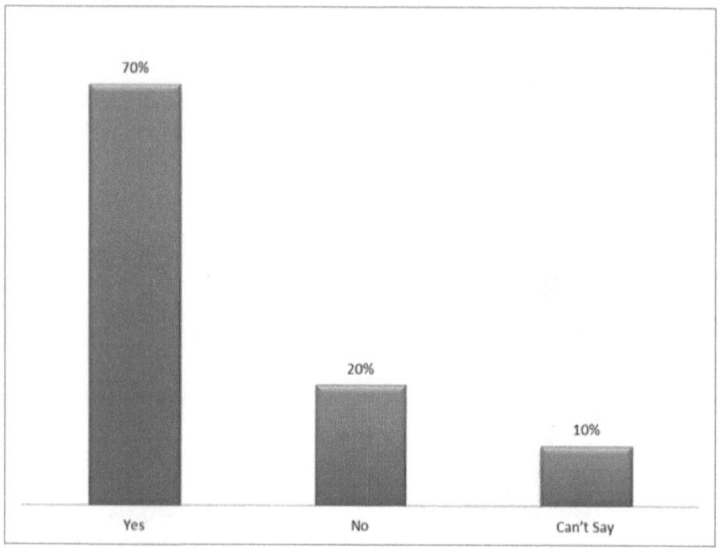

Analysis:-

In the response of question no.A14, almost 70% employees say yes and 20% say no. It means that there is 70-20% thinking of people and more survival on short term issue then T&D issue is effect the HRD in SME.

CHAPTER-7

HUMAN RESOURCE MANAGEMENT- CHALLENGES AND SYNCHRONIZING VALUABLE RESOURCES

Dynamic

HR is the most important and one of kind resources of an association. The fruitful administration of an association's HR is an energizing, dynamic and testing assignment, particularly when the world has turned into a worldwide town and economies are in a condition of motion. The shortage of skilled assets and the developing desires for the current laborer have additionally expanded the intricacy of the human asset work.

In this chapter we will examine significant difficulties in HRM and how the genuine administration of HR is considered as the obligation of the considerable number of directors in an association. We will likewise talk about the issues in human asset the executives in a changing situation and furthermore recommends conceivable methods for utilizing and overseeing HR.

7.1   Introduction

HRM is about how individuals are overseen by a business so as to meet the key targets of the business. The useful goals set for HRM should be predictable with the corporate targets. In the event that a business is to be fruitful and accomplish its targets, at that point it needs to deal with its HR viably. The job of HR supervisor has changed in light of social, monetary and political conditions and to propel in innovation and it is as yet growing progressively. The general significance of a large number of the exercises has changed as outside conditions have influenced the requirements of associations and it is as yet a dynamic region where the jobs and methods for sorting out the HR work proceed to change and create.

HRM is valuable not exclusively to association, yet the representatives working in that, and furthermore the general public on the loose increment the shot for a fruitful begin.

Orientation- It is fundamentally an individual's essential demeanor, convictions, or emotions in connection to a specific subject or issue. A viable introduction will-

1. Foster a comprehension of the grounds culture, its qualities, and its decent variety
2. Help the new worker make an effective acclimation to the new activity
3. Help the new representative comprehend her job and how she fits into the all-out association.

Preparing and Development-As a director, one of the key duties of supervisor is to build up the staff. Fast change requires a gifted, learned workforce with representatives who are versatile, adaptable, and concentrated on what's to come.

Execution Appraisal-: It is an efficient assessment of a person regarding act at work and person's potential for advancement. An exhibition the board exchange ought to be uncomplicated however nitty sufficiently gritty to give representatives a reasonable sign of what is expected of them in their occupations. The attention is on discourse. It is imperative when an act desire is set to decide how it will be estimated.

Following are alternate zones of HRM:

1. Career Planning
2. Compensation
3. Benefits
4. Labor Relations
5. Record-keeping

7.2   Diagnostics Model of HRM

It is additionally another instrument of picking up knowledge data of the association. In spite of the fact that, it shifts from association to association yet couple of strategies are regular in each diagnostics think about like-

1. Study of the Organization. Its framework, techniques, arrangement and method and so on.
2. Discussion with the best administration and key individuals
3. Interview of the workers from every division irrespective of their designation and levels.
4. Finding the gaps
5. Again dialog with the key individuals about the holes
6. Finding the solutions.
7. Implementation and execution of the solution.
8. Periodical Audits.

7.3   Arrangement MODEL

Incorporating the HR work with vital office objectives requires significant investment, steadiness, and an inside and out learning of the procedure included. The HRD/Organization Alignment Model appeared as follows, shows the way toward adjusting HRD with the HR work (HR) and the hierarchical arranging capacity.

The three dimensions in each square speak to the relationship among the association, HR and HRD capacities. A case of this relationship is appeared as follows:

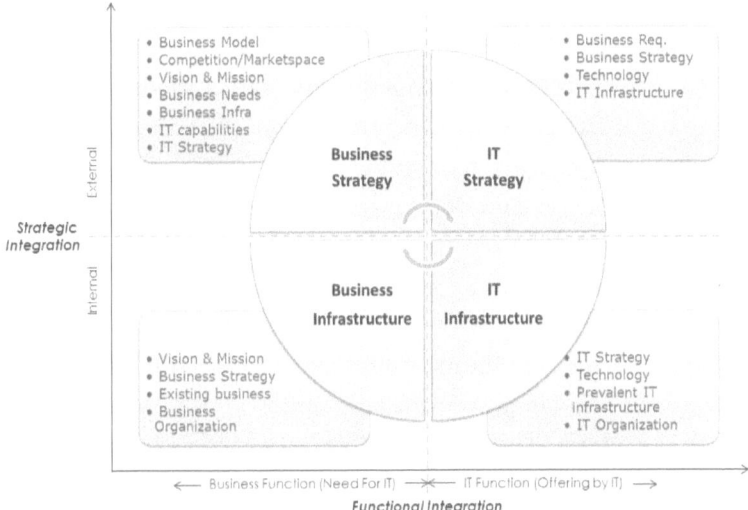

Figure

Associations can adjust HR to the business technique by directing a thorough indicative evaluation of HR's execution and utilizing the subsequent examination as the reason for procedure improvement and usage arranging.

METHODOLOGY

The attributes highlights of research approach utilized for the venture can be expressed as pursues:

1. The essential target of this investigation is to analyze hierarchical destinations as HRM is a way to accomplish productivity and adequacy.
2. HRM performs such huge numbers of capacities for different offices. In any case, it must see that the help ought not to cost more than the advantage rendered.
3. It is essential to coordinate offices and open doors for individual or gathering improvement with the development of the association.

4. Effective utilization of HR in the accomplishment of hierarchical objectives in another prime goal to analyze.
5. To distinguish and fulfill individual and gathering needs by giving satisfactory and impartial wages, motivators, worker advantages and government managed savings and measures for testing work, esteem, acknowledgment, security, status.
6. Maintaining high representatives' assurance and sound human relations by continuing and improving the different conditions and offices.
7. Appreciating the human resources consistently by giving preparing and improvement programs.
8. To consider and add to the minimization of financial wrongs, for example, joblessness, under-business, disparities in the dissemination of pay and riches and to improve the welfare of the general public by giving work chances to ladies and impeded areas of the general public.
9. To give a chance to articulation and voice the board.
10. To give reasonable, adequate and effective authority.

Other important subtleties in connection to look into procedure are as per the following-

While the exact HR targets will differ from business to business and industry to industry, the accompanying focuses are additionally generally observed as imperative HR goals.

1. Ensure HR is utilized expense successfully.
2. Make successful utilization of workforce potential.
3. Match the workforce to the business needs.
4. Maintain great business/worker relations. In any case, the key target of any association is survival. Associations are not simply happy with this objective. Hence in this paper our center is to look at the objective of the vast majority of the associations which is for the most part development and benefits.

PRIOR APPROACH

Over and over again, managers must deal with events that are clearly similar but also different enough to require fresh thinking. For example:

1. Businesses is expanding or failing.
2. They innovate or stagnate.
3. They may be exciting or unhappy organizations in which to work.
4. Finance has to be obtained.
5. Workers have to be recruited.
6. New equipment is purchased, eliminating old procedures and introducing new methods.
7. Staff must be reorganized, retrained or dismissed.

Some items in this paper are clearly listed with people management (for example, recruiting or reorganizing staff). Human resource management draws on many sources for its theories and practices. Sociologists, psychologists and management theorists, especially, have contributed a constant stream of new and reworked ideas. They offer theoretical insights and practical assistance in areas of people management such as recruitment and selection, performance measurement, team composition and organizational design. Many of their concepts have been integrated into broader approaches that have contributed to management thinking in various periods and ultimately the development of HRM (see Figure).

Huarte produced the following classification (Smith, 1948, p.11):

> **Part 3**
> **HRM - Areas of influence**
>
> HRM Systems directly influence:
> - Cost effective ways to recruit, manage and control the behaviors of the employees.
> - Development of human capital.
> - Employee behaviors and performance to give satisfactory and continuously improving performance
> - The organizational structure.
> - The achievement of the organization's goals.

1. Some have an aura for the unmistakable and simple parts, yet can't comprehend the dark and troublesome.
2. Some are malleable and simple, ready to become familiar with every one of the standards, however nothing more than a bad memory at contention.
3. Some need no instructors, they deplore the fields yet look for unsafe and high places and walk alone, pursue no beaten track; these must admission forthwith, agitated, trying to know and see new issues.

OUR APPROACH

1. After investigating HRM in detail, the examination uncovers to offers minimal solid direction to rehearsing administrators on the way toward creating HR—and with regards to a vital arrangement.
2. The in general reason for the human asset the board work must concentration to upgrade the individual and aggregate commitment of representatives to the achievement of the association.
3. The generally speaking motivation behind human asset the board should empower an association to improve the individual and aggregate commitments of workers to the accomplishment of the

association. As of late, human asset capacities have extended and turned out to be progressively unpredictable. In the meantime, there has been a developing accentuation on guaranteeing that human asset rehearses fit with the key bearing of the association.

The issue of vital HRM at first came to unmistakable quality around the mid-1990s, at which time scholastics created meanings of key HRM as:

1. The endeavor of each one of those exercises influencing the conduct of people in their endeavors to plan and execute the vital needs of business.
2. The example of arranged human asset organizations and exercises expected to empower the association to accomplish its objectives an association can't assemble a decent group of working experts without great Human Resources. HR views workers as its inward clients and renders administrations considering that. The principle and essential target of the HR the board is utilizing the salaried staff in an association adequately and healthy for the association's advantages. On account of this beneficial workplace, association can achieve its objectives and proceed with its capacities.

Like Armstrong (2006), Barutçugil (2004) additionally managed the points of the HRM and he characterized these points comparably. A typical point underscored by these specialists is acquiring hierarchical objectives through the worker. As indicated by Barutçugil (2004), HRM points **(as cited in Aray, 2008, p.4):**

1. To help all workers achieve ideal execution and to utilize completely their ability and potential,
2. To persuade representatives to apply more exertion for achieving hierarchical objectives,

3. To utilize HR in an ideal method to achieve authoritative objectives,
4. To live up to workers' vocation desires and advancement,
5. To bring together authoritative plans and HR techniques and make and keep up a corporate culture,
6. To offer a workplace animating shrouded innovativeness and vitality,
7. To make work conditions invigorating development, collaboration, and absolute quality idea.
8. To energize adaptability for accomplishing learning association. As it is referenced above, being interrelated with all divisions and outer condition makes HRM a substantially more perplexing framework, and HRM rehearses progressively accept new obligations that are connected with associations. For that r

END

The examination on Human Resource Management Practices has raised various discoveries about the execution and the board of individuals. A portion of the discoveries in this exploration calls attention to very obviously the impact of sound HRM framework in an organization. There are some different discoveries and perceptions that best utilization of HR prompt the advancement, both monetary just as social. While the financial advancement prompts business extension and broadening alongside high rates of benefits, the social improvement prompts high occupation fulfillment level, high class business morals and qualities among workers. It likewise prompts the famously and rating of a Company.

The motivation behind this investigation was to comprehend the arrangements identified with HRM utilize that is set up at associations with territories of tasks. The way to incorporated human asset arranging in the division going ahead is to keep the procedure uncomplicated, and in this manner, expanding its helpfulness. All the above discoveries are the general in nature, which mirror the dynamic standpoint of the organization. 48% of managers battle to locate the correct applicants as indicated by Manpower.

Overview:- Absence of accessible hopefuls, specialized abilities among that present, refusal to move to another area, poor picture of the occupation, powerless delicate aptitudes and interest for a higher pay have been key reasons in Asia Pacific for the presents on stay empty. The discoveries demonstrate that the organization is following e- Enlistment practice, which is a standout amongst the best known, rehearses in its classification. All enlistment in Executive and Non Executives at acceptance level is based on e- Enrollment process. HR professionals in an independent company who have balanced mastery give various administrations to workers. The zones in which HR keeps up control can enhance employees' perception of HR all through the workforce when they trust HR considers representatives to be its inside clients and renders administrations in view of that.

Mr. Diminish F. Drucker has properly watched the criticalness of work force as directors are found of rehashing the Trusim that the main genuine contrasts between one association and the other the execution of individuals.

Fundamentally, the manager improvement and execution of an association despite the fact that not exclusively but rather intensely depend on the nature of work force.

Last however not the least; a human asset the executive's framework, or HRMS, ought to includes the largest amount of human asset the board exercises. The program of different human asset arrangements ought to be inside steady in connection to a human asset objective. HRMS is likewise the coordination of human asset the executives and data innovation to computerize and encourage human asset exercises.

The general thought of a HRMS enables private company directors to create reasonable human asset frameworks dependent on their field of business also, business development arranges. The worldwide world is never again just a wellspring of new markets or cost factor investment funds; it is a wellspring of advancement. Any association, without an appropriate setup for HRM will undoubtedly experience the ill effects of major issues while dealing with its standard exercises.

Hence, today, organizations must put a great deal of exertion and vitality into setting up a solid and successful HRM.

CHAPTER-8

THE CONGRUENCE MANAGEMENT -A DIAGNOSTIC TOOL TO IDENTIFY PROBLEM AREAS IN A COMP

Abstract: The congruence management model is a diagnostic tool that evaluates how well the elements within an organization work together and how they can be better integrated to improve performance. Chronological age is often used as a proxy for defining the wants and needs of consumers. This paper will represent how environment and person interacts with each other and discuss how it can aid in explaining the individual needs of aging consumers that need to be met to allow for successful aging. Outcomes for product design, service environments, and technological solutions will also be discussed. In this paper several internal elements are mentioned by which a company transforms input, such as resources, into output, such as goods or services. The paper will also highlight the basic premise of the congruence management model in which the betterment of a company's basic internal elements works together and how faster it attains its goals.

8.1   Introduction

Goal congruence is the term which describes the situation when the goals of different interest groups coincide. A way of helping to achieve goal congruence between shareholders and managers is by the introduction of carefully designed remuneration packages for managers which would motivate managers to take decisions which were consistent with the objectives of the shareholders.

8.1.1   The Congruence Model-Aligning the Drivers of High Performance

Why does one organization seem to thrive on a certain corporate structure or type of work, while another struggles to make a profit?

The answer lies in understanding the key causes or drivers of performance and the relationship between them. The Congruence

Model, first developed by David A Nadler and M L Tushman in the early 1980s, provides a way of doing just this.

It's a powerful tool for finding out what's going wrong with a team or organization, and for thinking about how you can fix it.

Several unanswered questions arise, like:-

1. Is your organization's performance as good as it could be?
2. What could be changed to improve things and why would this help?
3. Does the key lie in the work itself?
4. Or with the people doing it?
5. Should you reorganize the corporate structure? Or try to change the prevailing culture?

This model, developed by David Nadler and Michael Tushman at Columbia University, is often used in business management to identify problem areas within a company and focuses on several broad elements: the work a company does; the people who do it; the structure of the company; and its culture as mentioned above.

8.1.2   How to Achieve Goal Congruence

Goal congruence can be achieved, and at the same time, the 'agency problem' can be dealt with, providing managers with incentives which are related to profits or share price, or other factors such as:

1. Pay or bonuses related to the size of profits termed as profit-related pay.
2. Rewarding managers with shares, e.g.: when a private company 'goes public' and managers are invited to subscribe for shares in the company at an attractive offer price.

Such measures might encourage management in the adoption of "creative accounting" methods which will distort the reported performance of the company in the service of the managers own ends. However, creative accounting methods such as off-balance sheet finance present a temptation to management at all times given that they allow a more favorable picture of the state of the company to be presented than otherwise, to shareholders, potential investors, potential lenders and others. An alternative approach is to attempt to monitor manager's behavior.

For example - By establishing 'Management audit' procedures, to introduce additional reporting requirements, or to seek assurance from managers that shareholders' interests will be foremost in their priorities.

8.2   Literature Review

8.2.1   The Congruence Model for Organization Analysis

The Nadler-Tushman Congruence Model is a more comprehensive model, specifying inputs, throughputs, and outputs, which is consistent with open systems theory (Katz & Kahn, 1978). The model is based on several assumptions which are common to modern organizational diagnostic models;

These assumptions are as follows: -

1. Organizations are open social systems within a larger environment.
2. Organizations are dynamic entities (i.e., change is possible and occurs).
3. Organizational behavior occurs at the individual, the group, and the systems level.
4. Interactions occur between the individual, group, and systems levels of organizational behavior.

These assumptions have been used in some of the previous models examined, although only implicitly. The inputs within the Nadler-Tushman Congruence model include such factors as the environment, resources, history (i.e., patterns of past behavior), and organizational strategies. Nadler and Tushman are explicit in their conceptualization of each of the factors.

For example, they describe the resources available to the organization as human resources, technology, capital, information, and other less tangible resources. While strategy is an input in the model, it is the single most important input to the organization and is depicted by the arrow from the input box to the organization. The system components of the whole organizational transformation process are informal organizational arrangements, task, formal organizational arrangements, and individual components. Similarly; the outputs of the model include individual, group, and system outputs: products and services, performance, and effectiveness. While outputs such as products and services are generally understood.

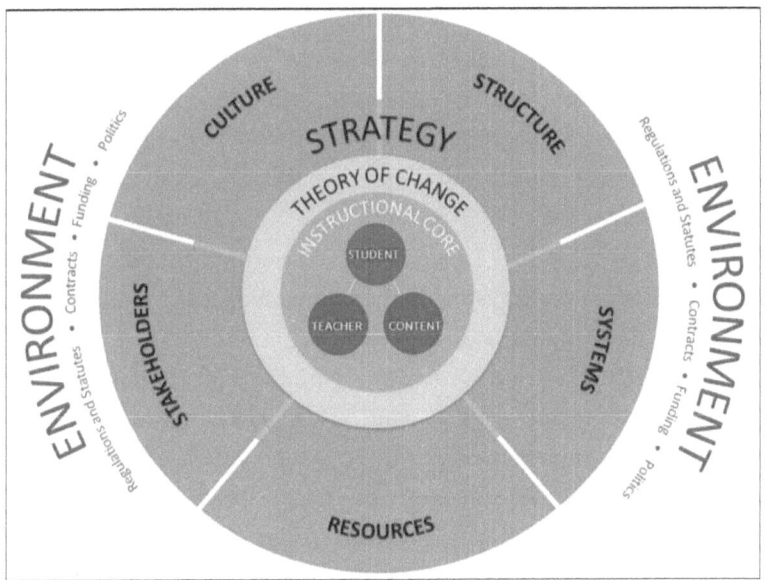

Figure 1. Components of the Congruence Model.

Organizations are effective when the four key components of performance – tasks, people, structure, and culture – fit together. When these elements work in unison to support and promote high performance, the end result is an organization wide system that functions efficiently and effectively.

When pieces are out of synch with each other, the friction that is caused has a negative impact on the entire process, which limits the overall productivity that can be achieved.

This makes Congruence Analysis a useful tool for fixing problems in your team or organization. Use it to take a look at the organizational components contributing to your overall performance, and create congruence in and between them – people will be much more satisfied and the work will be done that much more effectively.

8.2.2 The Congruence Model-Culture

The culture of a company consists of its politics, values, behavior patterns and rules - including the unwritten ones. These are examined in light of how well, or how poorly, they support the company's overall goals and fit with other elements. If the formal structure of a company has ceased to be relevant, the informal structure, or culture, often supplants it. Sometimes the culture of a company needs to change in order to improve performance or to adapt to a new business focus. For example, a relaxed, creative corporate culture may work well within a new startup company, but may need to become more conservative as the company grows.

Most of the literature on implementation of Enterprise Resource Planning (ERP) systems focuses upon identification of critical success factors, which fails to cater for the complex and integrative nature of ERP implementation. This study provides a comprehensive explanation of inter-relationships of a variety of factors at play during ERP implementation using Nadler's Congruence Model (Nadler and Tushman, 1980) and Roggers' Diffusion of Innovation Model (Roggers, 1983). Results verify Nadler's proposition of complex inter-relationships of organizational components. For example, communication about ERP implementation impacts skills and knowledge, creates a collaborative environment, reduces uncertainty and increases exposure through training. The collaborative work culture created through communication further impacts skills and knowledge as well as formal coordination between departments. The aforementioned facilitators were further found to impact decision to use the system by affecting the stages proposed by Roggers, i.e. awareness, perceived value and motivation. Overall, communication was found to be the most important factor throughout implementation. Thus ERP implementation requires subsequent changes in all of organizational elements, and success can only be guaranteed if these elements are in harmony with each other.

Dr. Paul T. P Wong in the resource–congruence model posits that coping is effective to the extent that appropriate resources are available and congruent coping strategies are employed. According to him the model emphasizes the importance of developing resources in anticipation of exigencies, and the need for acquiring cultural knowledge as to what coping strategies are suitable for a given stressor.

8.3   Research Methodology

In order for researchers to understand and predict behavior, they must consider both person and situation factors and how these factors interact. Even though organization researchers have developed interactional models, many have Overemphasized both person or situation components, and most have failed to consider the effects that persons have on situations. This paper presents criteria for improving interactional models and a model of person-organization fit, which satisfies these criteria. Using a Q-sort methodology, individual value profiles are compared to organizational value profiles to determine fit and to predict changes in values, norms, and behaviors.

8.3.1 Person–Environment Fit (P–E Fit)

It is defined as the degree to which individual and environmental characteristics match (Dawis, 1992; French, Caplan, & Harrison, 1982; Kristof-Brown, Zimmerman, & Johnson, 2005; Muchinsky & Monahan, 1987). Person characteristics may include an individual's biological or psychological needs, values, goals, abilities, or personality, while environmental characteristics could include intrinsic and extrinsic rewards, demands of a job or role, cultural values, or characteristics of other individuals and collectives in the person's social environment (French et al., 1982). Due to its important implications in the workplace, person– environment fit has maintained a prominent position in Industrial and organizational psychology and related fields (for a review of theories that address person-environment fit in organizations, see Edwards, 2008).

Person–environment fit can be understood as a specific type of person–situation interaction that involves the match between corresponding person and environment dimensions (Caplan, 1987; French, Rodgers, & Cobb, 1974; Ostroff & Schulte, 2007). Even though person–situation interactions as they relate to fit have been discussed in the scientific literature for decades, the field has yet to reach consensus on how to conceptualize and operationalize person–environment fit. This is due partly to the fact that person–environment fit encompasses a number of subsets, such as person–supervisor fit and person–job fit, which are conceptually distinct from one another (Edwards & Shipp, 2007; Kristof, 1996). Nevertheless, it is generally assumed that person– environment fit leads to positive outcomes, such as satisfaction, performance, and overall well-being (Ostroff & Schulte, 2007).

8.3.2   Diagnostic Models

Diagnostic models typically involve a series of steps that ultimately get to the root cause of a problem. Although there are several common models for analyzing performance in the workplace, including (Cable, 2008) process mapping system, arguably the most well-known is A. C. Daniels's ABC analysis model, which capitalizes on changing components of the three-term contingency.

8.3.3   Q-Methodology (Also Known as Q-Sort)

This is the systematic study of participant viewpoints. Q-methodology is used to investigate the perspectives of participants who represent different stances on an issue, by having participants rank and sort a series of statements

Figure 2. *Q-sort Methodology.*

Participant responses are analyzed using factor analysis. Unlike standard uses of factor analysis (often called R Methodology), the variables are individuals not traits. There are five basic steps in setting up this methodology:-

1.   Definition of the domain of discourse on the particular issue;
2.   Development of the set of statements (Q-sort);
3.   Selection of the participants representing different perspectives;

4. Q sort by participants; and
5. Analysis and interpretation.

Q-sort is a mixed methodology. It uses the qualitative judgments of the researcher in defining the problem, developing statements to investigate the perspectives of participants (some of the statements may be developed after interviewing key informants), and selecting participants. It uses quantitative options of analysis. It can be very helpful in unearthing perspectives without requiring participants to articulate these clearly themselves. It is a useful complement to a range of other objective evaluation measures. For example, Q-methodology can be used to examine teacher's perspectives on teaching as part of an evaluation of a school district. Other evaluation measures can include test scores, attendance and completion.

8.4   Discussion

The arrangement of the structural elements may need to be updated to make them mesh well with other elements within the company or a changing business environment. If the company's leadership culture changes -- a chief executive officer retires and is replaced by a younger leader, for example -- the company's culture has changed.

Applying the congruence model could be a long and expensive process, especially for global organizations with several business units and thousands of employees. The model does not specify a direct way for incorporating group dynamics into organizational analysis. The absence of a structured template, while giving managers flexibility, might also limit their ability in quickly coming up with proven solutions to organizational problems. The application of this model may exclude the possibility that the absence of a fit does not necessarily imply a problem because there may not always be a perfect fit between tasks and individuals, especially in small entrepreneurial companies. However, this should not limit effectiveness because companies have to adapt continually to changes. For example, training and mentoring programs could bring new employees up to speed on new responsibilities.

Jolita Vveinhardt, Evelina Gulbovaitė, Congruence model of personal and organizational values presents in his article which recommends congruence model of personal and organizational values expedience as well as benefit are described and problem areas of personal and organizational values congruence in Lithuanian organizations that he highlighted in his paper. Congruence model of personal and organizational values consists of a sequence of stages:-

1. In the first phase the needs are adjusted, i.e. when there is a need for staff in the organization – they start looking for a suitable candidate to occupy the position of the work.
2. The second phase maybe realized in 2 ways: so that to set the match of values between the organization and the employees in it as well as during personnel selection – to set the match between the values of the organization and the candidates.
3. In the third phase the grade of congruence of values is established.
4. In the fourth stage tools to strengthen congruence of values are chosen.
5. In the fifth stage the above chosen tools are applied.
6. In the sixth stage the impact of the tools on the employees is studied.
7. In the seventh stage decisions concerning further strengthening of values congruence are taken.

8.5   Conclusion

The higher the compatibility (congruence) amongst these elements, the higher the organizational performance will be. If the elements are incongruent then organizational performance will not be optimal, and the organizational design will need to be amended to change this.

The congruence model provides a rigorous framework for analyzing complex organizational problems. It is a tool for thinking through organizational problems, not a rigid template for classifying observations. It does not specify a particular approach for designing organizational structures or processes as long as there is a fit between the various components. The model also helps companies think through the impact of change management on organizational interactions and performance. The social components -- people and informal structures and technical components, tasks and formal structures -- must fit as part of the congruence model. For example, if the product manager is not on speaking terms with the marketing manager, there could be design delays and poor market penetration.

The implementation of the congruence model involves identifying the symptoms of problems, determining the gaps between inputs and outputs, describing the fit between an organization's components, identifying problem areas and developing an action plan to deal with these problems.

The application of this model may exclude the possibility that the absence of a fit does not necessarily imply a problem because there may not always be a perfect fit between tasks and individuals, especially in small entrepreneurial companies. However, this should not limit effectiveness because companies have to adapt continually to changes. For example, training and mentoring programs could bring new employees up to speed on new responsibilities.

CHAPTER-9

CONCLUSION

In total, we state that human asset improvement and preparing can overhaul the nature of individuals. With the utilization of arrangement instruments from people in general part, a domain for lifetime learning can be made. This gives motivations to little and medium undertakings to acknowledge the preparation of individuals so they can legitimately react to the adjustment in the outside condition. Hence, we have four as a dream for human asset advancement and preparing for little and medium endeavors train the proprietors of little and medium ventures to legitimately take control of the new economy patterns and new learning in the board with which they can plan new worldwide activity models for supported business task. Sustain a gathering of seed-instructors with universal perspectives to help little and medium ventures to give careful consideration to human asset the executives and advancement. By at that point, they will most likely oversee undertakings and build up inward preparing framework so as to update the nature of representatives. Quicken the overhauling and change of customary businesses and train little and medium undertakings to create optional aptitudes. Help to prepare business visionaries to enhance work in the nation. Get up to speed with the information society; support center and senior officials with the idea of lifetime learning so as to cut out learning associations.

The examination and elucidation of information on investigation of HRD in Small and Medium Enterprises" that specialist (we) discovered Results of polls demonstrate that HRD in little and medium ventures has such huge numbers of factor which impact – work turnover, terrible social and authoritative culture, poor preparing structure, less create human asset data framework, stress the board strategies of representatives, tutoring strategy of worker, official legislative issues of representative and the executives, absence of inside HRD mindfulness, proprietor/administrator numbness of human asset arrangements, absence of instructive preparing and improvement between the executives proprietor, more survivals on transient issue by the administration.

Result demonstrates that the social and hierarchical culture of little and medium endeavors isn't great. In little and medium association the work turnover is additionally high. The structure of an association is exposed to some type of changes intermittently and it would be infertile with culture. Subsequently, unmistakably the authoritative culture and endeavors to change and oversee it are genuine worry of H.R.M. Culture might be social or authoritative, is connected to system and structure and impact exercises, for example, enlistment, determination, examination, preparing, and remunerates. In any case, in SME the social and hierarchical culture isn't great. This is likewise reason of high work turnover.

Result appears in SME's no one offers consideration regarding the student and the learner structure. Preparing builds the learning and ability of a representative. Preparing enhances changes conduct and frame of mind of workers. Each kind of occupation more often than not requires some preparation for proficient execution. Workers ability are insufficient just and completely profitable without a methodical preparing program. Because of less or no preparation workers has not completely built up their potential and they are not given their 100% to the association.

From the study analyst found that in these enterprises work turnover is more whether it is identified with laborer level or staff level. Workers are not completely fulfilled from HR strategies. They are not feel cheerful working. They feel the social just as hierarchical culture isn't great. They feel pressure when they work that is the reason they are not give their 100% in the work. In the vast majority of the association no preparation is given and whenever gave in some association it's insufficient. The pay framework isn't great and they feel that they are not getting full cash of their work.

There are proof to help a huge selection of HR rehearses in associations, it gives the idea that organizations won't seek after all part of HR rehearses in the meantime and all things considered, needs will be given to specific methods emphasize on collaboration could get significant underwriting at a specific minute in the time and different exercises could be retired for the present.

There was little proof to substantiate the connection between corporate system and HR methodology. The absence of this connection was likewise found in sizable number of association in review, when following practices were contemplated: worker and the board advancement, representative connection and hierarchical improvement.

All in all, the HR exercises are basic for SMEs for long haul survival. HR exercises, for example, preparing and improvement, profession arranging, self-coordinated learning, representative inspiration have driven towards a superior execution, higher imagination and advancement, holding staff, better administration and balance and enhance human capital. It is trusted that little firms should make procedures to improve learning, aptitudes, and mastery. As far as HRD, these have prompted better execution and energized individual for higher duty to the hierarchical execution. In the present HRD, it is vital for all measured association and with no uncommon for little firms also.

We trust, in light of the above vision and bearings, to prepare proficient corporate administration advisors with present day the board abilities and worldwide perspectives to make appropriate enhancements of monetary positions, overhaul the productivity of budgetary administration and focused intensity of little and medium undertakings under the exertion of the legislature.

REFERENCES

1. How to Change with the Congruence Management Model, By Mary Strain

2. Concept of goal congruence, Published on June 22, 2016, https://www.linkedin.com/pulse/concept-goal-congruence-etinosa-aca-acfe-amscce-clrmp-ifrs-cert

3. the Congruence Model-Aligning the Drivers of High Performance, By the MindTools ContentTeam, https://www.mindtools.com/pages/article

4. Improving Interactional Organizational Research: A Model of Person-Organization Fit, Jennifer A. Chatman[1]

5. Person–environment fit, Wikipedia, the free encyclopedia

6. http://www.betterevaluation.org/en/evaluation-options/qmethodology

7. Congruence Model, https://leg4.wikispaces.com/Congruence+Model

8. Pros and Cons of the Congruence Model, *by Chirantan Basu,* http://smallbusiness.chron.com/pros-cons-congruence-model

9. ERP Implementation: An Application of Nadler's Congruence Model, Neelab Kayani, FAST School of Management, Sadia Nadeem

10. Effective management of life stress: The resource–congruence model, Dr Paul T. P Wong, volum e 9, Issue 1 January 1993, Pages 51–60

11. (2011, 2). Congruence Model Researchomatic. Retrieved 2, 2011, from http://www.researchomatic.com/Congruence-Model-62184.html, Congruence Model

12. Congruence model of personal and organizational values, Jolita Vveinhardt, Evelina Gulbovaitė, ISSN 1822-6760. Management theory and studies for rural business and infrastructure

development. 2012. Vol. 33. NR. 4. ND STUDIES FOR RURAL BUSINESS AND INFRASTRUCTURE DEV ELOPMENT.

13. Chabra T.N. "Human Resource Management", Vikas publishing house, Delhi, 5th Edition, 2004.

14. Bernardin H. John "Human Resource Management", Tata McGraw Hill Publication, 8th Edition 2010. //

15. Bhatnagar Jyotsna, Budhkar Pawan S. (2009) "Changing face of people management in India" Sterling book house.

16. Mukherjee Kumkum "Principal of Management", Tata McGraw Hill Publication, 2nd Edition 2009.

17. Ivancevich John "Human Resource Management", Tata McGraw Hill Publication, 9th Edition 2003.

18. Singh A.K., (2008) "Managing People", Excel book publication.

19. Bolar, Malati, (1979) "Performance Appraisal" Vikas publishing house, New Delhi.

20. Ivancevich John & Lee Soo "Human Resource Management in Asia", Tata McGraw Hill Publication, 1st Edition 2002.

21. Sherlekar S.A. and Sherlekar V.S., (2008) "Modern Business Organisation and Management" Himalaya Publishing House.

22. Tripati P.C., Reddy P.N. "Principal of Management" Tata McGraw-Hill, 4th Edition, 2008.

23. Beardwell I., Holden L. 2001. Human Resources Management, a Contemporary Approach, 3rd Edition, Ed. Financial Times Pretince Hall, United Kingdom,

24. Wayne Cascio "Managing Human Resource", Tata McGraw Hill Publication, 6th Edition 2002.

25. Saha Tapash "Business Organisation & Management", Tata McGraw Hill Publication, 1st Edition 2009.

26. Thirumalai ramaraju, (2008) "Resource management for Sustainable Development" Himalaya Publishing House.

27. Monga J.R., Financial Accounting: Concept & Applications, Mayur Paperbacks, 19th Edition.

28. Bhatia S.K. (2006) "Human resource management: A competitive Advantage" Sterling Book house.

29. Hollenbeck John, Noe Raymond, Gerhart Barry & Patrick "Fundamentals of Human Resource Management", Tata McGraw Hill Publication, 1st Edition 2004.

30. Howell, David C. 1997, Statistical Methods for Psychology, 4th edition. Duxbury Press, London,

31. Lussier Robert "Human Relation in Organization", Tata McGraw Hill Publication, 6th Edition 2004.

32. Rao P.Subba, (2008) "Business Policy and Strategic management" Himalaya publishing house.

33. Pandey I.M., Financial Management, Vikas Publishing House Pvt. Ltd. 8th Edition.

34. Nambudiri Ranjeet & Cascio Wayne "Managing Human Resource", Tata McGraw Hill Publication, 8th Edition 2010.

35. Rao P.Subba "Personnel and Human Resource Management" Himalaya publishing house, 2008.

36. Mintzberg H. 2004. Managers, not MBAs: a hard look at the soft practice of managing and management development, 1 Edition, Ed. Berrett-Koehler Publishers, 2004.

37. Glueck, William F. Personnel; a Diagnostic Approach, 3rd Edition Plano, Inc. 1982.

38. Katz Harry, Kochan Thomas "An Introduction to Collective Bargaining & Industrial Relations", Tata McGraw Hill Publication, 3rd Edition 2003.

39. Bhattacharyya Deepak Kumar (2001) "Human Resource Planning", Excel Book Publication, 3rd Edition.

40. Khandelwal N. M. (2007) "Indian Ethos and value for managers" Himalaya publishing house.

41. Eisner Alan, Lumpkin G.T. & Dess Gregory "Strategic Management", Tata McGraw Hill Publication, 1st Edition 2004.

42. Kazmi Azhar, "Strategic Management and Business Policy", Tata McGraw Hill Publication, 3rd Edition 2008.

43. Kothari C.R., "Research Methodology" Methods & Techniques, 2ⁿᵈ edition, New Age International (P) Ltd., 2003.

44. Noe Raymond "Employee Training and Development", Tata McGraw Hill Publication, 3ʳᵈ Edition 2004.

45. Burgelman Robert, Christensen Clayton & Wheelwright Steven, "Strategic Management of Technology & Innovation", Tata McGraw Hill Publication, 4ᵗʰ Edition 2009.

46. Punnett Jane Batty, (2004) "International perspective organisation behaviour human resource management" Sterling book house.

47. Werther William, Davis Keith "Human Resources and Personnel Management", Tata McGraw Hill Publication, 5ᵗʰ Edition 2003.

48. Sharma A.M. (2009) "Personnel and Human Resource Management" Himalaya publishing house.

49. Bhattacharyya D K "Human Resource Planning" Excel Books Publication, 2ⁿᵈ Edition.

50. Timmons Jeffry & Spinelli Stephen "New Venture Creation", Tata McGraw Hill Publication, 7ᵗʰ Edition 2009.

51. Alewine, Thomas C. "Performance Appraisal and Performance Standards" Personnel Journal, 1982.

52. Cravens David & Piercy Nigel "Strategic Marketing", Tata McGraw Hill Publication, 4ᵗʰ Edition 2009.

53. Deb Tapomoy (2007) "Compensation Management", Excel book publication, 1ˢᵗ Edition.

54. Walker Gordon "Modern Competitive Strategy", Tata McGraw Hill Publication, 1ˢᵗ Edition 2005.

55. Shermon Ganesh, (2007) "Knowledge Human Resource Management" Himalaya publishing house.

56. W.F.Cascio, "Managing Human Resources", New Delhi, Tata McGraw Hill, 2003.

57. R.J.Harvey, "Job Analysis" in M.D.Dunnette and L.M.Hough (ed.), Handbook of industrial and organisational psychology, Palo Alto, C.A., Consulting psychologists press, 1991.

58. Mukherjee Kumkum "Principal of Management and Organizational Behaviour", Tata McGraw Hill Publication, 2nd Edition 2009.

59. CAIIB (2010) "Human resource management" Sterling book house.

60. Lussier Robert "Human Relation in Organization", Tata McGraw Hill Publication, 5th Edition 2002.

61. Bhanushal S.G. (2006) "Managing twenty first century organisation" Himalaya publishing house.

62. Michelle Brown, Walsh Janet, Plowman D. & Deery S. " Industrial Relation", Tata McGraw Hill Publication, 2nd Edition 2001.

63. G.Dessler, "Human Resource Management", New Delhi, Prentic Hall of India, 2004.

64. Davis Keith, Werther William "Human resource and Personnel Management", Tata McGraw Hill Publication, 5th Edition 1996.

65. Sutherland J., Canwell D. 2004, Key Concepts in Human Resource Management, Ed. Palgrave Macmillan, New York.

66. Appannaiah, Reddy and Anita (2005) "Personnel and human resource management", Himalaya publishing house.

67. H.J.Bernardin, "Human Resource Management", New Delhi, Tata McGraw Hill, 2003.

68. Ackloff, Russel L., The Design of Social Research, chicango; University of Chicago Press, 1961.

69. Saha Jayantee (2009), "Management and Organizational Behaviour", Excel Books Publication, 1st Edition.

70. Menon P.K.S. (2005), "Human resource management and Organisational Behaviour" Himalaya publishing house.

71. Wheelwright Steven, Christensen Clayton & Burgelman Robert "Strategic Management of Technology and Innovation", Tata McGraw Hill Publication, 4th Edition 2004.

72. Mittal Shweta & Bhatia Kanchan (2005) "Manpower Development for Technological Change", Excel books publication, 1st Edition.

73. Bailey, Kenneth D., "Methods of Social Research," New York, 1978.

74. Sterman John "Business Dynamics", Tata McGraw Hill Publication, 1st Edition 2004.

75. Reddy B.Rathan (2007) "Effective human resource training and development strategy" Himalaya publishing house.

76. Best, John W., and Kahn, James V., "Research in Education," 5th Ed., New Delhi; Prentice-Hall of India Pvt. Ltd. 1986.

77. Kothari, C.R., Quantitative Technique, 2nd ed., New Delhi: Vikas Publishing House Pvt. Ltd., 1984.

78. Arthur, M. and Hendry, C. (1990) 'Human resource management and the emergent strategy of small to medium sized business units', International Journal of Human Resource Management.

79. Megginson William L., Byrd Mary Jane & Megginson Leon "Small Business Management", Tata McGraw Hill Publication, 4th Edition 2004.

80. Menon P.K.S. (2009), "Human resource management" Himalaya publishing house.

81. Beaver, G., & Hutchings, K. (2005). Training and developing an age diverse workforce in SMEs: The need for a strategic approach, Education & Training.

82. Balakrishnan Lalita, Srividhya S. (2008) "Human resource development" Himalaya publishing house.

83. Freel Mark & Deakins David "Entrepreneurship and Small Firms", Tata McGraw Hill Publication, 3rd Edition 2004.

84. Westhead, P. and Storey, D. (1996). Management training and small firm performance: why is the link so weak? International Small Business Journal, Vol. 14,

85. Abel, M.H. (2008). Competence management and learning organizational memory: Journal of knowledge management. 12, (6), 12-30.

86. Bartlett, A.C., and S. Ghoshal, 2002. Building competitive advantage to human resource through people: MIT Sloan management review 41.

87. HR Executive Editorial Survey (2002); Workplace Turnover study, Human resource executive magazine.

88. Jones Gareth & George Jennifer "Contemporary Management", Tata McGraw Hill Publication, 5th Edition 2009.

89. French, Kartz, & Rosenweig; Understanding human behaviour in organization, New York, Harper & Row.

90. Birch, D. (1998) 'HR and understanding small and medium-sized enterprises', Human Resource Development International.

91. Stacey, R. D. (1990) 'Dynamic strategic management', in M. Armstrong (ed.) The New Manager's Handbook, London: Kogan Page.

92. Hill, R. and Stewart, J. (1999) 'HRD in small organisations', Human Resource Development International.

93. McGoldrick J., Stewart J., Watson S. (2001) 'Theorizing human resource development', Human Resource Development International.

94. Westhead P. and Storey D. J. (1996) "Management training and small firm performance: why is the link so weak?" International Small Business Journal.

95. Sambrook, S. (2000) 'Talking of HRD', Human Resource Development International.

96. https://www.shrm.org/shrm-india/pages/how-can-indian-small-and-medium enterprisesbridge-the-digital-skill-challenges.aspx

97. https://www.peoplematters.in/article/sme-talent/challenges-for-hr-in-smes-14956

98. How to Change with the Congruence Management Model, By Mary Strain

99. Concept of goal congruence, Published on June 22, 2016, https://www.linkedin.com/pulse/concept-goal-congruence-etinosa-aca-acfe-amscce-clrmp-ifrs-cert
100. the Congruence Model-Aligning the Drivers of High Performance, By the MindTools ContentTeam, https://www.mindtools.com/pages/article
101. Improving Interactional Organizational Research: A Model of Person-Organization Fit, Jennifer A. Chatman[1]
102. Person–environment fit, Wikipedia, the free encyclopedia

WEBSITES:

www.google.com
www.humanresources.about.com
www.hrsolutions.com
www.citehr.com
www.performancemanagmentguide.com
www.jobdescription.com
www.smeindia.net
www.smeindia.org
www.msme.gov.in

APPENDICES

(Questionnaires)

A) Which factor effect the HRD in SME?

1)	Social & organizational culture	y/n
2)	Personnel policy	y/n
3)	Recruitment and selection policy	y/n
4)	Training structure	y/n
5)	Performance appraisal policy	y/n
6)	Grievances	y/n
7)	HR information system	y/n
8)	Stress management policy	y/n
9)	Mentoring	y/n
10)	Official politics	y/n
11)	Employee training.	y/n
12)	Lack of internal HR awareness.	y/n
13)	Less educated owner/management.	y/n
14)	More survival on short term issues then T&D issues.	y/n

LIST OF PAPER PUBLISHED IN NATIONAL & INTERNATIONAL JOUNRAL

www.ijemr.net

ISSN (ONLINE): 2250-0758, ISSN (PRINT): 2394-6962

Volume-5, Issue-6, December-2015

International Journal of Engineering and Management Research

Page Number: 555-559

Human Resource Management-Challenges and Synchronising Valuable Resources

Ms Almas Sabir

MIS Department, College of Business Administration, University of Hail, Kingdom of SAUDI ARABIA

ABSTRACT

Human resources are the most valuable and unique assets of an organization. The successful management of an organization's human resources is an exciting, dynamic and challenging task, especially at a time when the world has become a global village and economies are in a state of flux. The scarcity of talented resources and the growing expectations of the modern day worker have further increased the complexity of the human resource function.

In this paper we will discuss major challenges in HRM and how the actual management of human resources is considered as the responsibility of all the managers in an organization. We will also discuss the issues in human resource management in a changing environment and also suggests possible ways of leveraging and managing human resources.

Keywords— Challenges, Human Resource Management, Objectives

I. INTRODUCTION

HRM is about how people are managed by a business in order to meet the strategic objectives of the business. The functional objectives set for HRM need to be consistent with the corporate objectives. If a business is to be successful and achieve its objectives, then it needs to manage its human resources effectively. The role of HR manager has changed in response to social, economic and political conditions and to advances in technology and it is still developing dynamically. The relative importance of many of the activities has changed as external circumstances have affected the needs of organizations and it is still a dynamic area where the roles and ways of organizing the HR function continue to change and develop.

HRM is useful not only to organization, but the employees working therein, and also the society at large

also find it useful. The human resources division of any company has the daunting task of ensuring that the company has the best and most effective workforce possible. For this reason the human resources division plays a vital role in any company, and especially when it comes to the overall employee satisfaction and their well-being. It is therefore imperative that the Human Resources department have a finger on the pulse at all times when it comes to the company's goals and objectives, and that they are able to constantly look at new ways to keep the employees happy, motivated and on the right track..

Literature review deals with the following areas of HRM-
Human Resource Planning- Ensures the right people with the right skills at the right time and adequate human resources to meet the strategic goals and operational plans of the organization. The basic questions to be answered for strategic planning are:

1. Where are we going?
2. How will we develop HR strategies to successfully get there, given the circumstances?
3. What skill sets do we need?

Job Analysis- It is a process to identify and determine in detail the particular job duties and requirements and the relative importance of these duties for a given job. Job analysis's a process where judgments are made about data collected on a job. Following are the areas encompassed by job analysis:

1. What to do
2. How to do
3. Why to do it
4. Qualifications

Staffing- Most companies have a mission statement. This outlines the purpose of the company, why it exists, its goals and values and what it wants to achieve. Organizational staffing involves ensuring that all new positions advertised will fit with those company goals to benefit the business. The time spend in planning for the new person's first days and weeks on the job will greatly increase the chance for a successful start.

Orientation- It is basically a person's basic attitude, beliefs, or feelings in relation to a particular subject or issue. An effective orientation will-

1. Foster an understanding of the campus culture, its values, and its diversity
2. Help the new employee make a successful adjustment to the new job
3. Help the new employee understand her role and how she fits into the total organization.

Training and Development- As a manager, one of the key responsibilities of manager is to develop the staff. Rapid change requires a skilled, knowledgeable workforce with employees who are adaptive, flexible, and focused on the future.

Performance Appraisal-: It is a systematic evaluation of an individual with respect to performance on the job and individual's potential for development. A performance management discussion should be uncomplicated but detailed enough to give employees a clear indication of what is required of them in their jobs. The focus is on dialogue. It is important when a performance expectation is set to determine how it will be measured.

Following are the other areas of HRM:

1. Career Planning
2. Compensation
3. Benefits
4. Labor Relations
5. Record-keeping

Diagnostics Model of HRM is also another tool of gaining insight information of the organization. Although, it varies from organization to organization but few methods are common in every diagnostics study like-
1- Study of the Organization. Its system, methods, policy and procedure etc.
2- Discussion with the top management and key people
3- Interview of the employees from each department irrespective of their designation and levels.
4- Finding the gaps
5- Again discussion with the key people about the gaps
6- finding the solutions.
7- Implementation and execution of the solution
8 -Periodical Audits.

ALIGNMENT MODEL

Integrating the HR function with strategic agency goals takes time, persistence, and an in depth knowledge of the process involved. The HRD/Organization Alignment Model, shown below, illustrates the process of aligning HRD with the human resources function (HR) and the organizational planning function.

The three levels in each block represent the relationship among the organization, HR, and HRD functions. An example of this relationship is shown below through one block of the model.

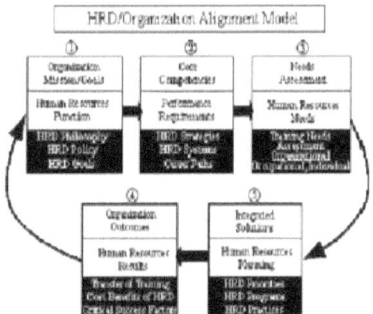

Organizations can align HR with the business strategy by conducting a rigorous diagnostic assessment of HR's performance and using the resulting analysis as the basis for strategy development and implementation planning.

II.   METHODOLOGY

The characteristics features of research methodology used for the project can be stated as follows:

1. The primary objective of this study is to examine organizational objectives as HRM is a means to achieve efficiency and effectiveness.
2. HRM performs so many functions for other departments. However, it must see that the facilitation should not cost more than the benefit rendered.
3. It is important to match facilities and opportunities for individual or group development with the growth of the organization.
4. Effective use of human resources in the achievement of organizational goals in another prime objective to examine.
5. To identify and satisfy individual and group needs by providing adequate and equitable wages, incentives, employee benefits and social security and measures for challenging work, prestige, recognition, security, status.
6. Maintaining high employees' morale and sound human relations by sustaining and improving the various conditions and facilities.
7. Appreciating the human assets continuously by providing training and development programs.
8. To consider and contribute to the minimization of socio-economic evils such as unemployment, under-employment, inequalities in the distribution of income and wealth and to improve the welfare of the society by providing employment

opportunities to women and disadvantaged sections of the society.

9. To provide an opportunity for expression and voice management.
10. To provide fair, acceptable and efficient leadership.

Other necessary details in relation to research methodology are as follows-

Whilst the precise HR objectives will vary from business to business and industry to industry, the following points are also commonly seen as important HR objectives-

1. Ensure human resources are employed cost-effectively.
2. Make effective use of workforce potential.
3. Match the workforce to the business needs.
4. Maintain good employer / employee relations.

However, the fundamental objective of any organization is survival. Organizations are not just satisfied with this goal. Therefore in this paper our focus is to examine the goal of most of the organizations which is mainly growth and profits.

III.   PRIOR APPROACH

Over and over again, managers must deal with events that are clearly similar but also different enough to require fresh thinking.
For example:

1. Businesses is expanding or failing.
2. They innovate or stagnate .
3. They may be exciting or unhappy organizations in which to work.
4. Finance has to be obtained.
5. Workers have to be recruited.
6. New equipment is purchased, eliminating old procedures and introducing new methods .
7. Staff must be reorganized, retrained or dismissed.

Some items in this paper are clearly listed with people management (for example, recruiting or reorganizing staff). Human resource management draws on many sources for its theories and practices. Sociologists, psychologists and management theorists, especially, have contributed a constant stream of new and reworked ideas. They offer theoretical insights and practical assistance in areas of people management such as recruitment and selection, performance measurement, team composition and organizational design. Many of their concepts have been integrated into broader approaches that have contributed to management thinking in various periods and ultimately the development of HRM (see Figure).

Part 3
HRM - Areas of influence

HRM Systems directly influence:

■ Cost effective ways to recruit, manage and control the behaviors of the employees.

■ Development of human capital.

■ Employee behaviors and performance to give satisfactory and continuously improving performance

■ The organizational structure.

■ The achievement of the organization's goals.

Huarte produced the following classification (Smith, 1948, p.11):

1. Some have a disposition for the clear and easy parts, but cannot understand the obscure and difficult.
2. Some are pliant and easy, able to learn all the rules, but no good at argument.
3. Some need no teachers, they take no pleasure in the plains but seek dangerous and high places and walk alone, follow no beaten track; these must fare forthwith, unquiet, seeking to know and understand new matters.

IV.   OUR APPROACH

1. After analyzing HRM in detail, the study reveals to offers little concrete guidance to practicing managers on the process of developing human resources—and in the context of a strategic plan.
2. The overall purpose of the human resource management function must focus to enhance the individual and collective contribution of employees to the success of the organization.
3. The overall purpose of human resource management should enable an organization to enhance the individual and collective contributions of employees to the success of the organization. In recent years, human resource functions have expanded and become more complex. At the same time, there has been a growing emphasis on ensuring that human resource practices fit with the strategic direction of the organization.

4. One way of looking at the various aspects of human resource management is seen in the diagram below-

The issue of strategic HRM initially came to prominence around the early 1990s, at which time academics developed definitions of strategic HRM as:

1. The undertaking of all those activities affecting the behavior of individuals in their efforts to formulate and implement the strategic needs of business.
2. The pattern of planned human resource deployments and activities intended to enable the organization to achieve its goals

An organisation cannot build a good team of working professionals without good Human Resources. HR considers employees to be its internal customers and renders services with that in mind. The main and primary objective of the human resources management is using the salaried staff in an organization effectively and salutary for the organization's benefits. Thanks to this productive work environment, organization can reach its goals and continue its functions.

Like Armstrong (2006), Barutçugil (2004) also dealt with the aims of the HRM and he defined these aims in a similar way. A common point emphasized by these researchers is obtaining organizational goals through the employee. According to Barutçugil (2004), HRM aims (as quoted in Aray, 2008, p.4):

1. To help all employees reach optimal performance and to use fully their capacity and potential,
2. To convince employees to exert more effort for reaching organizational goals,
3. To use human resources in an optimum way to reach organizational goals,
4. To meet employees' career expectations and development,
5. To unify organizational plans and HR strategies and create and maintain a corporate culture,
6. To offer a working environment stimulating hidden creativity and energy,
7. To create work conditions stimulating innovation, teamwork, and total quality concept.
8. To encourage flexibility for achieving learning organization. As it is mentioned above, being interrelated with all departments and external environment makes HRM a much more complex system, and HRM practices increasingly assume new responsibilities that are related with organizations. For that r

V. CONCLUSION

The study on Human Resource Management Practices has brought up a number of findings about the performance and management of people. Some of the findings in this research points out very clearly the effect of sound HRM system in a company. There are some other findings and observations that best use of human resources leads to the development, both economic as well as social. While the economic development leads to business expansion and diversification along with high rates of profits, the social development leads to high job satisfaction level, high class business ethics and values amongst employees. It also leads to the popularly and rating of a Company.

The purpose of this study was to understand the policies related to HRM use that is in place at organizations with areas of operations. The key to integrated human resource planning in the department going forward is to keep the process uncomplicated, and in so doing, increasing its usefulness. All the above findings are the general in nature, which reflect the progressive outlook of the company. 48% of employers struggle to find the right candidates according to Manpower Survey. Lack of available candidates, technical competencies amongst that present, refusal to move to another location, poor image of the occupation, weak soft skills and demand for a higher salary have been key reasons in Asia Pacific for the posts to remain vacant. The findings show that the company is following e-

Recruitment practice, which is one of the best known practices in its category. All recruitment in Executive and Non Executives at induction level is based on e-Recruitment process. HR practitioners in a small business who have well-rounded expertise provide a number of services to employees. The areas in which HR maintains control can enhance employees' perception of HR throughout the workforce when they believe HR considers employees to be its internal customers and renders services with that in mind.

Mr. Peter F. Drucker has rightly observed the significance of personnel as managers are found of repeating the Trusim that the only real differences between one organization and the other the performance of people. In essence, the supervisor development and performance of an organization although not solely but heavily depend on the quality of personnel.

Last but not the least, a human resource management system, or HRMS, should encompasses the highest level of human resource management activities. The program of multiple human resource policies should be internally consistent in relation to a human resource objective. HRMS is also the integration of human resource management and information technology to automate and facilitate human resource activities. The general notion of an HRMS helps small-business managers craft suitable human resource systems based on their field of business and business growth stage. The global world is no longer simply a source of new markets or cost factor savings; it is a source of innovation. Any organization, without a proper setup for HRM is bound to suffer from serious problems while managing its regular activities. For this reason, today, companies must put a lot of effort and energy into setting up a strong and effective HRM.

REFERENCES

[1] Human resource management J. Coyle-Shapiro, K. Hoque, I. Kessler, A. Pepper, R. Richardson and L. Walker, 2013

[2] The Impact of Human Resource Management on Organizational Performance: Progress and Prospects Brian Becker[1] and Barry Gerhart[2]

[3] Human Resources Management: Some New Directions,Gerald R. Ferris[1],Wayne A. Hochwarter[2], M. Ronald Buckley[3],Gloria Harrell-Cook[4] and Dwight D. Frink[5]

[4] Rickard, C. and A. Boroughs (2009) Dos and Don'ts in a downturn, People Management, 15 January, 38–9.

[5] Key Human Resources Objectives, Susan Kihn

[6] Human Resource Management and Its Importance for Today's Organizations Zehra Alakoç Burma, PhD, Edu. Assistant Professor Higher Vocational School of Mersin Mersin University Mersin, Turkey.

Journal of Political Science and International Relations
2018; 1(2): 34-38
http://www.sciencepublishinggroup.com/j/jpsir
doi: 10.11648/j.jpsir.20180102.11

The Congruence Management -a Diagnostic Tool to Identify Problem Areas in a Company

Almas Sabir

College of Business Administration, University of Hail, Hail, Kingdom of Saudi Arabia

Email address:
almas.sabir083@gmail.com

To cite this article:
Almas Sabir. The Congruence Management -a Diagnostic Tool to Identify Problem Areas in a Company. *Journal of Political Science and International Relations*. Vol. 1. No. 2. 2018, pp. 34-38. doi: 10.11648/j.jpsir.20180102.11

Received: December 3, 2017; Accepted: December 12, 2017; Published: January 29, 2018

Abstract: The congruence management model is a diagnostic tool that evaluates how well the elements within an organization work together and how they can be better integrated to improve performance. Chronological age is often used as a proxy for defining the wants and needs of consumers. This paper will represent how environment and person interacts with each other and discuss how it can aid in explaining the individual needs of aging consumers that need to be met to allow for successful aging. Outcomes for product design, service environments, and technological solutions will also be discussed. In this paper several internal elements are mentioned by which a company transforms input, such as resources, into output, such as goods or services. The paper will also highlight the basic premise of the congruence management model in which the betterment of a company's basic internal elements works together and how faster it attains its goals.

Keywords: Congruence Management, Internal Elements, Diagnostic Approach, Structure, Culture

1. Introduction

Goal congruence is the term which describes the situation when the goals of different interest groups coincide. A way of helping to achieve goal congruence between shareholders and managers is by the introduction of carefully designed remuneration packages for managers which would motivate managers to take decisions which were consistent with the objectives of the shareholders.

1.1. The Congruence Model-Aligning the Drivers of High Performance

Why does one organization seem to thrive on a certain corporate structure or type of work, while another struggles to make a profit?

The answer lies in understanding the key causes or drivers of performance and the relationship between them. The Congruence Model, first developed by David A Nadler and M L Tushman in the early 1980s, provides a way of doing just this.

It's a powerful tool for finding out what's going wrong with a team or organization, and for thinking about how you can fix it.

Several unanswered questions arise, like:-

1. Is your organization's performance as good as it could be?
2. What could be changed to improve things and why would this help?
3. Does the key lie in the work itself?
4. Or with the people doing it?
5. Should you reorganize the corporate structure? Or try to change the prevailing culture?

This model, developed by David Nadler and Michael Tushman at Columbia University, is often used in business management to identify problem areas within a company and focuses on several broad elements: the work a company does; the people who do it; the structure of the company; and its culture as mentioned above.

1.2. How to Achieve Goal Congruence

Goal congruence can be achieved, and at the same time, the 'agency problem' can be dealt with, providing managers with incentives which are related to profits or share price, or other factors such as:

1. Pay or bonuses related to the size of profits termed as profit-related pay;

2. Rewarding managers with shares, e.g.: when a private company 'goes public' and managers are invited to subscribe for shares in the company at an attractive offer price.

Such measures might encourage management in the adoption of "creative accounting" methods which will distort the reported performance of the company in the service of the managers own ends. However, creative accounting methods such as off-balance sheet finance present a temptation to management at all times given that they allow a more favorable picture of the state of the company to be presented than otherwise, to shareholders, potential investors, potential lenders and others. An alternative approach is to attempt to monitor manager's behavior.

For example - By establishing 'Management audit' procedures, to introduce additional reporting requirements, or to seek assurance from managers that shareholders' interests will be foremost in their priorities.

2. Literature Review

2.1. The Congruence Model for Organization Analysis

The Nadler-Tushman Congruence Model is a more comprehensive model, specifying inputs, throughputs, and outputs, which is consistent with open systems theory (Katz & Kahn, 1978). The model is based on several assumptions which are common to modern organizational diagnostic models;

These assumptions are as follows: -

1. Organizations are open social systems within a larger environment.

2. Organizations are dynamic entities (i.e., change is possible and occurs).

3. Organizational behavior occurs at the individual, the group, and the systems level.

4. Interactions occur between the individual, group, and systems levels of organizational behavior.

These assumptions have been used in some of the previous models examined, although only implicitly. The inputs within the Nadler-Tushman Congruence model include such factors as the environment, resources, history (i.e., patterns of past behavior), and organizational strategies. Nadler and Tushman are explicit in their conceptualization of each of the factors.

For example, they describe the resources available to the organization as human resources, technology, capital, information, and other less tangible resources. While strategy is an input in the model, it is the single most important input to the organization and is depicted by the arrow from the input box to the organization. The system components of the whole organizational transformation process are informal organizational arrangements, task, formal organizational arrangements, and individual components. Similarly, the outputs of the model include individual, group, and system outputs: products and services, performance, and effectiveness. While outputs such as products and services are generally understood.

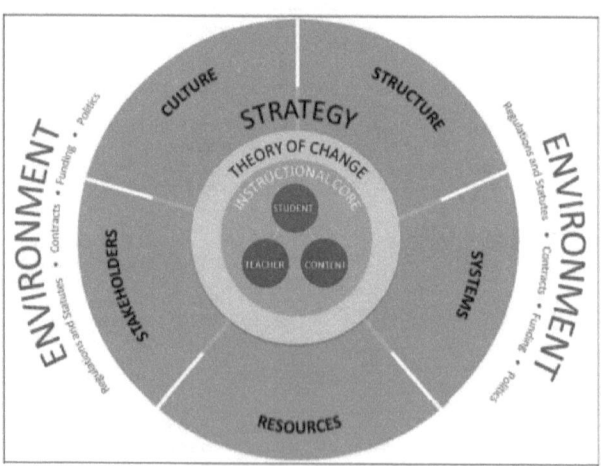

Figure 1. Components of the Congruence Model.

Organizations are effective when the four key components of performance – tasks, people, structure, and culture – fit together. When these elements work in unison to support and promote high performance, the end result is an organization-wide system that functions efficiently and effectively.

When pieces are out of synch with each other, the friction that is caused has a negative impact on the entire process, which limits the overall productivity that can be achieved.

This makes Congruence Analysis a useful tool for fixing problems in your team or organization. Use it to take a look at the organizational components contributing to your overall performance, and create congruence in and between them – people will be much more satisfied and the work will be done that much more effectively.

2.2. The Congruence Model-CULTURE

The culture of a company consists of its politics, values, behavior patterns and rules - including the unwritten ones. These are examined in light of how well, or how poorly, they support the company's overall goals and fit with other elements. If the formal structure of a company has ceased to be relevant, the informal structure, or culture, often supplants it. Sometimes the culture of a company needs to change in order to improve performance or to adapt to a new business focus. For example, a relaxed, creative corporate culture may work well within a new startup company, but may need to become more conservative as the company grows.

Most of the literature on implementation of Enterprise Resource Planning (ERP) systems focuses upon identification of critical success factors, which fails to cater for the complex and integrative nature of ERP implementation. This study provides a comprehensive explanation of inter-relationships of a variety of factors at play during ERP implementation using Nadler's Congruence Model (Nadler and Tushman, 1980) and Roggers' Diffusion of Innovation Model (Roggers, 1983). Results verify Nadler's proposition of complex inter-relationships of organizational components. For example, communication about ERP implementation impacts skills and knowledge, creates a collaborative environment, reduces uncertainty and increases exposure through training. The collaborative work culture created through communication further impacts skills and knowledge as well as formal coordination between departments. The aforementioned facilitators were further found to impact decision to use the system by affecting the stages proposed by Roggers, i.e. awareness, perceived value and motivation. Overall, communication was found to be the most important factor throughout implementation. Thus ERP implementation requires subsequent changes in all of organizational elements, and success can only be guaranteed if these elements are in harmony with each other.

Dr. Paul T. P Wong in the resource–congruence model posits that coping is effective to the extent that appropriate resources are available and congruent coping strategies are employed. According to him the model emphasizes the importance of developing resources in anticipation of exigencies, and the need for acquiring cultural knowledge as to what coping strategies are suitable for a given stressor.

3. Research Methodology

In order for researchers to understand and predict behavior, they must consider both person and situation factors and how these factors interact. Even though organization researchers have developed interactional models, many have

overemphasized both person or situation components, and most have failed to consider the effects that persons have on situations. This paper presents criteria for improving interactional models and a model of person-organization fit, which satisfies these criteria. Using a Q-sort methodology, individual value profiles are compared to organizational value profiles to determine fit and to predict changes in values, norms, and behaviors.

3.1. Person–Environment Fit (P–E Fit)

It is defined as the degree to which individual and environmental characteristics match (Dawis, 1992; French, Caplan, & Harrison, 1982; Kristof-Brown, Zimmerman, & Johnson, 2005; Muchinsky & Monahan, 1987). Person characteristics may include an individual's biological or psychological needs, values, goals, abilities, or personality, while environmental characteristics could include intrinsic and extrinsic rewards, demands of a job or role, cultural values, or characteristics of other individuals and collectives in the person's social environment (French et al., 1982). Due to its important implications in the workplace, person-environment fit has maintained a prominent position in Industrial and organizational psychology and related fields (for a review of theories that address person-environment fit in organizations, see Edwards, 2008).

Person–environment fit can be understood as a specific type of person–situation interaction that involves the match between corresponding person and environment dimensions (Caplan, 1987; French, Rodgers, & Cobb, 1974; Ostroff & Schulte, 2007). Even though person–situation interactions as they relate to fit have been discussed in the scientific literature for decades, the field has yet to reach consensus on how to conceptualize and operationalize person–environment fit. This is due partly to the fact that person–environment fit encompasses a number of subsets, such as person–supervisor fit and person–job fit, which are conceptually distinct from one another (Edwards & Shipp, 2007; Kristof, 1996). Nevertheless, it is generally assumed that person–environment fit leads to positive outcomes, such as satisfaction, performance, and overall well-being (Ostroff & Schulte, 2007).

3.2. Diagnostic Models

Diagnostic models typically involve a series of steps that ultimately get to the root cause of a problem. Although there are several common models for analyzing performance in the workplace, including (Cable, 2008) process mapping system, arguably the most well-known is A. C. Daniels's ABC analysis model, which capitalizes on changing components of the three-term contingency.

3.3. Q-Methodology (Also Known as Q-Sort)

This is the systematic study of participant viewpoints. Q-methodology is used to investigate the perspectives of participants who represent different stances on an issue, by having participants rank and sort a series of statements

Figure 2. Q-sort Methodology.

Participant responses are analyzed using factor analysis. Unlike standard uses of factor analysis (often called R-Methodology), the variables are individuals not traits. There are five basic steps in setting up this methodology:-

1. Definition of the domain of discourse on the particular issue;
2. Development of the set of statements (Q-sort);
3. Selection of the participants representing different perspectives;
4. Q sort by participants; and
5. Analysis and interpretation.

Q-sort is a mixed methodology. It uses the qualitative judgments of the researcher in defining the problem, developing statements to investigate the perspectives of participants (some of the statements may be developed after interviewing key informants), and selecting participants. It uses quantitative options of analysis. It can be very helpful in unearthing perspectives without requiring participants to articulate these clearly themselves. It is a useful complement to a range of other objective evaluation measures. For example, Q-methodology can be used to examine teacher's perspectives on teaching as part of an evaluation of a school district. Other evaluation measures can include test scores, attendance and completion.

4. Discussion

The arrangement of the structural elements may need to be updated to make them mesh well with other elements within the company or a changing business environment. If the company's leadership culture changes -- a chief executive officer retires and is replaced by a younger leader, for example -- the company's culture has changed.

Applying the congruence model could be a long and expensive process, especially for global organizations with several business units and thousands of employees. The model does not specify a direct way for incorporating group dynamics into organizational analysis. The absence of a structured template, while giving managers flexibility, might also limit their ability in quickly coming up with proven solutions to organizational problems. The application of this model may exclude the possibility that the absence of a fit does not necessarily imply a problem because there may not always be a perfect fit between tasks and individuals, especially in small entrepreneurial companies. However, this should not limit effectiveness because companies have to adapt continually to changes. For example, training and mentoring programs could bring new employees up to speed on new responsibilities.

Jolita Vveinhardt, Evelina Gulbovaité, Congruence model of personal and organizational values presents in his article which recommends congruence model of personal and organizational values expedience as well as benefit are described and problem areas of personal and organizational values congruence in Lithuanian organizations that he highlighted in his paper. Congruence model of personal and organizational values consists of a sequence of stages:-

1. In the first phase the needs are adjusted, i.e. when there is a need for staff in the organization – they start looking for a suitable candidate to occupy the position of the work.
2. The second phase maybe realized in 2 ways: so that to set the match of values between the organization and the employees in it as well as during personnel selection – to set the match between the values of the organization and the candidates.
3. In the third phase the grade of congruence of values is established.
4. In the fourth stage tools to strengthen congruence of values are chosen.
5. In the fifth stage the above chosen tools are applied.
6. In the sixth stage the impact of the tools on the employees is studied.
7. In the seventh stage decisions concerning further strengthening of values congruence are taken.

5. Conclusion

The higher the compatibility (congruence) amongst these elements, the higher the organizational performance will be. If the elements are incongruent then organizational performance will not be optimal, and the organizational design will need to be amended to change this.

The congruence model provides a rigorous framework for analyzing complex organizational problems. It is a tool for thinking through organizational problems, not a rigid template for classifying observations. It does not specify a particular approach for designing organizational structures or processes as long as there is a fit between the various components. The model also helps companies think through the impact of change management on organizational interactions and performance. The social components -- people and informal structures and technical components, tasks and formal structures -- must fit as part of the congruence model. For example, if the product manager is not on speaking terms with the marketing manager, there could be design delays and poor market penetration.

The implementation of the congruence model involves identifying the symptoms of problems, determining the gaps between inputs and outputs, describing the fit between an organization's components, identifying problem areas and developing an action plan to deal with these problems.

The application of this model may exclude the possibility

that the absence of a fit does not necessarily imply a problem because there may not always be a perfect fit between tasks and individuals, especially in small entrepreneurial companies. However, this should not limit effectiveness because companies have to adapt continually to changes. For example, training and mentoring programs could bring new employees up to speed on new responsibilities.

References

[1] How to Change with the Congruence Management Model. By Mary Strain

[2] Concept of goal congruence. Published on June 22, 2016. https://www.linkedin.com/pulse/concept-goal-congruence-etinosa-aca-acfe-amscce-clmp-ifrs-cert

[3] the Congruence Model-Aligning the Drivers of High Performance. By the MindTools ContentTeam. https://www.mindtools.com/pages/article

[4] Improving Interactional Organizational Research: A Model of Person-Organization Fit. Jennifer A. Chatman[1]

[5] Person–environment fit, Wikipedia. the free encyclopedia

[6] http://www.betterevaluation.org/en/evaluation-options/qmethodology

[7] Congruence Model. https://leg4.wikispaces.com/Congruence+Model

[8] Pros and Cons of the Congruence Model. by Chitrantan Basu, http://smallbusiness.chron.com/pros-cons-congruence-model

[9] ERP Implementation: An Application of Nadler's Congruence Model. Neelab Kayani, FAST School of Management, Sadia Nadeem

[10] Effective management of life stress: The resource–congruence model. Dr Paul T. P Wong. volume 9, Issue 1 January 1993. Pages 51–60

[11] (2011. 2). Congruence Model Researchomatic. Retrieved 2. 2011, from http://www.researchomatic.com/Congruence-Model-62184.html. Congruence Model

[12] Congruence model of personal and organizational values. Jolita Vveinhardt. Evelina Gulbovaité. ISSN 1822-6760. Management theory and studies for rural business and infrastructure development. 2012. Vol. 33. Nr. 4. ND STUDIES FOR RURAL BUSINESS AND INFRASTRUCTURE DEVELOPMENT